POOL SIMPLIFIED, SOMEWHAT

George Fels

DOVER PUBLICATIONS, INC
Mineola, New York

Published in Canada by General Publishing Company, Ltd., 30 Lesmill Road, Don Mills, Toronto, Ontario.

Bibliographical Note

This book, first published by Dover Publications, Inc., in 2000, is an unabridged republication of *Pool Simplified—Somewhat,* originally published by Contemporary Books, Inc., in 1978.

Library of Congress Cataloging-in-Publication Data

Fels, George.
    Pool simplified, somewhat / George Fels.
       p. cm.
    Originally published: Chicago : Contemporary Books, c1978.
    Includes index.
    ISBN 0-486-41368-3 (pbk.)
     1. Pool (Game) I. Title.

GV891 .F44 2000
794.7'3—dc21

00-038413

Manufactured in the United States of America
Dover Publications, Inc., 31 East 2nd Street, Mineola, N.Y. 11501

Contents

Introduction   *vii*

1 Your cue   *1*

Sources; weight; thickness; straightness; tip; balance.

2 Your stance   *5*

Comfort; balance; the importance of level cue; the mechanical bridge.

3 Grip(s) and stroke(s)   *11*

Role of rear arm and bridge hand; bridges; stroke fundamentals; introduction to the cue ball; practice drills

4 Pocketing   *34*

Attitude; theory; aiming; the importance of center-ball play; introduction to pool's dual objectives; shotmaking and position drills; banks, caroms, and other puzzlements

5 Straight Pool   *61*

Theory; the opening break; playing the game; sequence; safeties; scratches; re-racking the balls.

6 Eight-Ball   *77*

The basic rules; the break; playing the game.

7 Nine-Ball   *81*

The rules; the break; playing the game.

8 Two others   *87*

Cribbage and Golf.

9 Game ball   *91*

Index   *93*

Introduction

Let me begin by complimenting you on your decision. In choosing pocket billiards (pool to us from now on) as a game which you'd like to learn, you've shown unparalleled wisdom. This could easily be one of the truly nifty recreational decisions of your life.

Pool is some game. It attracts nonathletes and excellent all-around athletes in strikingly close proportions; physical strength is no major factor, although it can't possibly hurt you to be in good physical condition for it. (The very best players are invariably good athletes, because pool is nothing more than hand/eye coordination, the basis of all sports.) At any level from beginner to champion, the game offers a relaxing, problem-solving sort of therapy, competitiveness, precision, skill, and chance.

It's also great fun.

One of my pet theories, and one that makes people look at me in a funny way, is that pool is more challenging than chess. Here's my rationale, and I promise you that if you keep playing this fabulous game for just a few weeks, you'll find yourself in total agreement:

1. It's equally infinite. No question about that. We're talking about 16 balls, each 2.25 inches in diameter, occupying 40.5 square feet of playing space on a regulation-size table. There is no pronounceable number for the number of patterns they can form.

2. Chess is pure concept; pool is concept plus execution. The pool player must make a choice of moves, as well thought out as he can make them; and then he has to complete the move he chooses. When round objects such as pool balls come in contact, only a pinpoint's worth of each actually touches, and that's the accuracy required to execute the move. Even on the easiest shots. In chess, of course your decision is a rich mental process, but once made, the piece can be moved for you with tongs if you like.

3. Pool offers no strategy specifically aimed at a draw. All major forms of pool create a winner, except for Rotation, a game fast becoming obsolescent.

4. There is no lore of previous grand masters on which to fall back when times get tough.

Don't be intimidated by this. As you become better at pool, you'll recognize that the real key to success is playing as *simply* as you can, no matter how complex your capabilities are. For that reason, and because pool does not require a great deal of you physically, pool *fundamentals* are especially critical. That's what this book is about. The closer you can stay to good fundamentals without adding unnecessary or unproductive embellishments, the better you'll do. We both want you to *grow* at the game, naturally, and there's a right way to do that. But a foundation built on flawed fundamentals will inhibit your pool progress more than I can ever tell you.

If you spend any time at all observing pool as well as playing it, you'll soon see that the game reflects the personalities of those who play it (although we're talking here about players whose seriousness about the game may exceed the pastime level). That might be something for you to consider, even at the beginner's stage, because it will help you see how important your *attitude* towards pool is. Get your head into this game; that is where the game of pool is largely played anyway. Play it indifferently and you'll have indifferent results.

Anyone in reasonably good health can look forward to enjoying pool for most of the rest of a lifetime. Since you have all that time and all that fun waiting for you, maybe we ought to begin.

POOL SIMPLIFIED, SOMEWHAT

1

Your cue

Let's change the pool subject from you to an extension of you. Skillfully used, that's just how a pool cue functions, communicating your ideas, judgment, and touch to the balls.

I can't tell you why, but for some reason a pool cue of one's own always seems to be a conversation-starter, far more than any other piece of sporting goods equipment I can think of. You never see an even moderately serious bowler without his own ball, or a golfer without his own clubs; and tennis players often take the court with a whole slew of rackets. Still, the notion of a personal, two-piece cue never fails to raise eyebrows or drop jaws.

Whatever people think, there are all kinds of good reasons for you to have your own cue, even as a beginner. It will help you immeasurably in gaining confidence and consistency. It will help you take the game more seriously. In short, it's just unarguable that having your own cue will make you a better player.

No need to overspend on this, either. All the country's top custom cue makers, who get $500 and up for their fanciest *objets d'art*, make excellent models for under $100. Sears', Ward's, and sporting goods stores sell even less expensive two-piece cues. Any of these cues will enhance your learning the game faster, although as you progress it's quite likely you'll become more demanding about what you want in a cue.

Three fine lines of mass-produced two-piece cues with which I'm familiar are the Viking cues, made in Madison, Wisconsin; the Palmer line, of Elizabeth, New Jersey; and the Adam cues, made in Japan by my friend Dick Helmstetter but widely distributed here. You'll find a broad spectrum of styles and prices among those suppliers (all of whom will work to your specifications on request), and you ought to find something to suit you.

If you want to aim your sights higher than that, the best custom cue makers now active include Danny Janes of Towson, Maryland, and Bill Stroud of Tulsa, Oklahoma, who were once partners and who both still make a cue called a Joss; Gus Szamboti of Penndel, Pennsylvania; Bert Schrager of Los Angeles; Bob Meucci of Memphis; and Burton Spain in Chicago.

But whether your cue comes off a cue maker's lathe or off the wall-rack in a commercial billiard room, here's what you want to look for.

Weight

Cues are generally made in the range of 16 to 22 ounces. But just about all players of note use cues weighing 19 or 20 ounces, or somewhere in between. The exception to this is that rare circumstance where a good player is forced to play with a house cue, and in that case the player will tend toward the heavier cues available, simply because they stay straighter longer. Experiment and see what feels good to you, but I think you'll find that 19 to 20 ounces is indeed the most practical playing range.

Thickness

Again, this is a matter of personal preference. Two cues can weigh exactly the same and still have demonstrably different tapers in both the butt (the bottom) and shaft (the length). Unlike a cue's weight, its specific taper plays no functional role in the stroke; it's simply what feels best to you that counts. Personally, I like a cue to feel slender both fore and aft; so I use a slightly longer cue than most players, but others like the heft of a real handful of cue. Twenty years ago, Gillette made a fortune off the identical principle, by offering three different weights of safety razor.

Straightness

A rainbow-shaped cue is obviously not going to help you much. The test for straightness could hardly be simpler: roll the cue on a table and look for wobbles (or, for that matter, *any* daylight between the two objects).

Tip

It's just a little bit of rubber or animal hide, but any good cue maker will tell you that the tip is where the making of a good cue begins. After all, that's where the action is. So be sure the tip of your cue is flush with the ferrule (that inch or so of white or black plastic just under the tip), with no bulge or droop over the edge like a Miami Beach midriff. And when selecting a house cue for play, check the amount of actual playing surface left on the tip. That means not the curved portion at the very top, but the cylindrical ridge between the top and the ferrule. A good healthy tip will stand at least an eighth of an inch off the ferrule before its slope begins. If the tip's contour arises immediately out of the ferrule, your tip is about to go to that great cue rack in the sky.

Keep that tip well chalked, too. Chalk helps the tip adhere to the ball during contact, and unless you have that, the ball squirts away at the damnedest angle and makes an awful sound and helps you lose. That's called a miscue. But chalk on your cue tip and a firm, level stroke are to miscues what the mongoose is to the cobra. Put that chalk on lovingly. "Like a broad puttin' on lipstick" is Minnesota Fats' simile for it. You move the chalk, not the cue.

Balance

Just as with taper, two cues of comparable weight can differ widely on where their precise balance points are. This is important because the balance point helps determine where your rear-hand grip will be. Find the point on the cue where you can balance it in your index and middle fingers without its tilting either way. That's the balance point, and the correct place for your grip is *generally* a foot, or slightly less, in back of that. I emphasize "generally" because many accomplished players hold their cues way, *way* back, sometimes actually touching the rubber butt protector at the very bottom. I don't recommend that you begin playing that way, but it does prove the validity of "different strokes for different folks." Again, see what feels best for you.

2

Your stance

For obvious reasons, learning the game of pool should include all the opportunities you can get to watch the best players you can find. And as you do that, there are enough good players around that I think you'll see a striking variance in stances.

Pool turns the offense over to you limitlessly when it's your turn at the table, and that makes it a very individualized game, indeed. Accordingly, different people will be comfortable in different stances simply because of their different bodies. The specific differences you'll see in stance are in placement of the feet and height of head over cue. And the best general instruction I can give you with respect to pool stance, at the risk of sounding permissive and immoral, is: *If it feels good, do it.* The objectives of the stance you do choose, and the common denominators between all those different experts' stances, are these; (1) comfort; (2) balanced, which comes as a matched set with comfort; and (3) a level cue.

I'll give you some general guidelines, but I'll go for any stance you can show me which accomplishes all three for you. None, of course, is worth a hang without the other two.

The old-timers used to teach stance in pool as if it were like the standing position in firing a rifle: feet spread at about shoulder width; feet, hands, head, and piece more or less in a line (Diagram 1). That makes sense on paper, except it doesn't allow for crouching, which every pool player must do but which no sane rifleman does. You can bend in that position, of course, but I hope to show you that that is not how you want your weight distributed.

Your stance should be such that you could withstand a theoretical shove on your rear shoulder without losing your balance. And I think if I were to stand you over the cue ball in that straight-line manner, bent as low or high as you please, you'd be vulnerable to the slightest pressure against your stance.

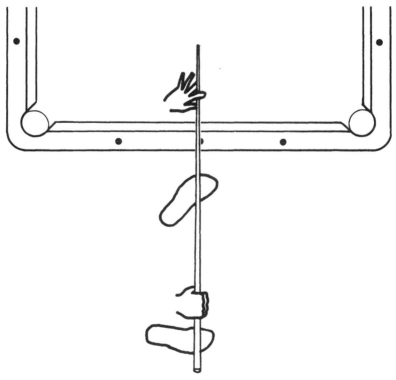

Diagram 1. Placement of hands, feet, and cue as traditionally taught.

Why worry about this when pool doesn't involve that kind of physical confrontation? Because the marvelous instruments called your brain and central nervous system tend to seek out balance automatically for you, and off-balance is simply not a natural way to stand. Proper stance will affect your comfort, which in turn will affect your concentration, and before you know it it's the other guy's turn.

You'll generally do better, I think, if you swing your lead foot somewhat out of the way, in the style of what baseball players call "stepping in the bucket" (Diagram 2). I know it's not the way to stand in the batter's box in baseball, but remember that baseball hitters do not attack a ball straight in front of them as pool players do; a pitch coming straight at a hitter cannot be hit at all. "Stepping in the bucket" is just what you want in pool; not only does it redistribute your weight more comfortably over the cue ball, but it also

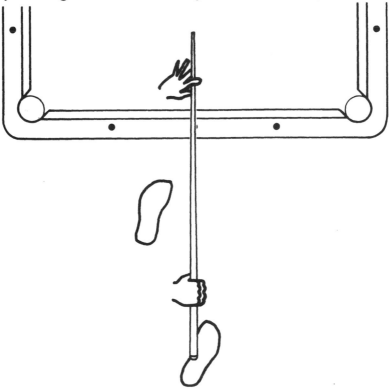

helps swing your rear hip clear of your stroking elbow. And that gets us right into objective number three, the level cue.

You can prove this to yourself without touching a cue. Just walk into any room and take note of how *few* players actually have their cues level—parallel to the table bed—during their strokes. Most of them will have the back end jacked up to some degree (some will be downright garish about this), and it has a great deal to do with their not standing correctly. If the room isn't busy, examine a table or two and see if you can find little pinholes in the felt. That's a result of the same thing: not holding the cue level.

A level cue is the one thing you can't do without in pool playing; you'll get nowhere, relatively speaking, without one. We'll get into the stroke itself in a while and take a further look at this. But it begins with your stance.

As to how high or low you stand over the cue, that is one more matter of personal comfort and preference. Both Willie Mosconi and Steve Mizerak, the dominant champions of their respective eras, assumed stances with their heads eight inches or so above their cues, so that might be a stance you'd want to try. If it doesn't feel quite right, all that means is that you won't be able to take a stance exactly like theirs. There'll still be one that feels good.

Another stance you'll benefit from testing is the one which gets you down as low over the cue as you can comfortably go. As a wearer of Coke-bottle-thick glasses, I believe in getting close to my work, and I can give you an even better reason than that: a substantial percentage of the best money players in the world show no daylight whatever between cue and chin. (For what it's worth, it also looks intimidating as hell, and you might as well learn from me as from an opponent that in pool, psyching is highly prevalent.)

A number of very advanced players have had success going to the open stance I propose for critical shots, on which they feel they need to bear down to the hilt, and going back to a more closed stance for the majority of their offense. But that's for later. What makes sense for now is for you to find a stance that is balanced, comfortable, and functional for you, and stick to it. Consistency of stance can be more elusive than you think, and you wouldn't believe the way in which a minor inadvertent change in your stance can change your game. That's why baseball hitters check their stance first—not their swings—whenever they detect a slump.

It's also worth noting that a substantial percentage of shots will not permit you to take your customary stance because they require your stretching to reach the cue ball. And a number of shots (typically, those in which a right-handed player must address the cue ball on the right-hand side of the table and cut a ball sharply to his left) will require you not only to stretch, but to shoot with the butt of your cue squarely under your belly. My advice for any of these stances and shots is quite simple: don't. Use the mechanical bridge (see below).

The rules of pool make it mandatory for you to keep one foot on the floor (or, as the wise guys say, both cheeks on the rail) no matter what your stance. I'm going to improve on that and suggest that while you're learning to play, *every one* of your shots should be engaged with *both* feet planted firmly, your weight balanced evenly and comfortably. And the way you accomplish that is to use the mechanical bridge, also called the rake, crutch, ladies' aid, and a number of barely printable epithets. Get comfortable with the bridge; it helps you reach every conceivable shot on the table, and used correctly, there's nothing sissified about it at all. The way bridge heads are made today, the bridge is easily as steady and dependable as your own hand. If you own your own table, try to get a device called the Russo Interlocking Bridge Head for your own equipment; if you play in a commercial room, do your best to have the Russos ordered and installed. Using this remarkable innovation is almost like being Plasticman, so effectively does it enhance your reach. But with or without the Russo Bridge Head, a superb habit for you to fall into early is to avoid stretching for pool shots. Stretching has absolutely no advantages; its disadvantages are to rob you of balance, comfort, power, and accuracy.

3

Grip(s) and stroke(s)

I can't give you quite the leeway on grips and strokes that I gave you on stance, although I'll grant that you'll find an occasional unorthodox style among successful players. That will hold true in just about all sports. No sane coach, for instance, would counsel a beginning boxer to fight with his hands at his sides, but it seems to work well enough for Muhammad Ali.

Still, I'd rate pool right under golf when it comes to the importance of correctness of fundamentals—stance, grip(s), stroke(s), and pocketing the object balls. Don't underestimate pool in this regard: if you can groove a consistent, correct, level stroke—just as in golf or tennis—you won't be a pool beginner for very long. From the physical point of view, it ought to be a piece of cake; all you're really doing is attacking an inert ball and rolling it a few feet, often less, on a smooth felt surface. But I think that getting the necessary fundamentals down correctly is really a test of discipline, and you don't get that from your body.

The game's physical simplicity, in fact, is exactly *why* you have to bear down on fundamentals. There's so little to do that the slightest little error anywhere along the line acts like a falling domino. Everybody makes these errors, of course; the game is played only by humans. (Ah there, Chess!) But it's consistency that makes the difference. The best players do the most things correctly more often.

All right. Now start thinking about all the nice things your hands have ever done for you. I don't intend to pry, but I want you to be thinking of your hands fondly. They, and your head, are your dearest pool friends, and they've got your head outnumbered.

We'll consider the butt, or stroking, hand first, because with rare exception, that hand does the same thing every single time; your bridge hand is going to have to learn some versatility.

The correct way to hold a pool cue is in the fingers and thumb. The butt of your cue and the palm of your hand should be, and remain, strangers. Your thumb should lie alongside the first joint of your index finger (Pictures 1 & 2).

Picture 1.

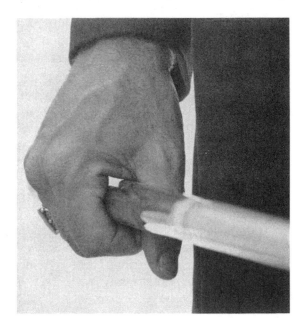

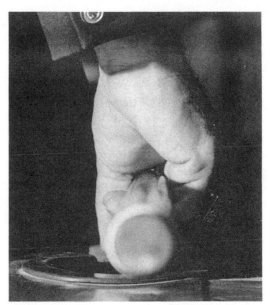

Picture 2.

The skin between your thumb and index finger may or may not touch the cue; that depends on the length of your fingers and how much pressure you need to exert on the cue to control your stroke. Either way, it's critical that you learn early to *cradle* the cue, rather than squeeze it. Too tight a grip will wreak all kinds of havoc upon your game and keep you from advancing; the game of pool just cannot be played that way. A death grip on the cue butt will, appropriately enough, kill the cue ball for you; and even though there are plenty of game situations in which you want to stop the cue ball dead, there's a comfortable and correct way to do that without strangling the cue.

The immortal Willie Hoppe taught that neither the ring nor little finger should ever touch the cue; the correct grip was executed by thumb and index and middle fingers, preferably thumb and index finger only. There is no reason to challenge Hoppe's wisdom, but I think you'll find more white rhinos in Texas than there are pool or billiards players who hold their cues that way today. It worked for him because both his stroke and the equipment on which he played were utterly flawless. Unless you can duplicate both conditions, I suggest you get all five fingers into the act.

The exception to that occurs when you want to use the mechanical bridge. In that case, the thumb and first two fingers are all you should use, as in Picture 3; you hold the cue just about as you would a pen. And your *left* hand does very little except to steady the butt of the bridge against the table or rail (Picture 4). By all means resist the temptation to lift the bridge butt up under your cue; that is umpteen times less firm and reliable than merely holding it in place down below.

It's in the shots you can reach comfortably that the left, or bridge, hand goes to work (reverse this, of course, if you're a lefty). And later we'll take a look at the various ways in which your left hand becomes functional.

If I were you, I'd make my beginning bridge very similar to Picture 5—and I'd never outgrow it, either. In fact, the more expert you become at the game, the more use you'll have for this bridge. It's ideal for simple shots which re-

Picture 3.

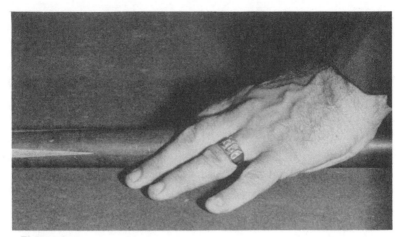

Picture 4.

Picture 5.

quire little or no cue-ball movement; it's the epitome of relaxation; it helps you discipline yourself against adding unnecessary or harmful embellishments to your stroke. The bridge which just about every advanced player in existence uses involves looping the forefinger over the cue shaft, and we're coming to that. But that same forefinger that's supposed to steady the cue can be as effective as any of Ma

Bell's cables when it comes to communicating any pressure you feel to your stroke. And if you play pool seriously at all, you'll find it brings a pressure all its own, one that does you no good.

So the open-thumb bridge is really a good friend to have. Another argument in its favor is that most champion snooker players use it, and snooker players are easily pool's finest shotmakers, driving little weeny balls into thankless, teeny little pockets on a table slightly less large than the size of the Houston Astrodome.

Keep your fingers together in forming this bridge. Cup your hand enough that your palm is raised off the table surface; the correct points of contact between hand and table are the heel of the hand, the butt of the thumb, and the four fingertips. The thumb rests firmly but comfortably against the second, or main, joint of the forefinger, and the cue rides gently and unencumbered over the ridge of the thumb.

The lone drawback to this bridge is rather obvious: there's nothing to prevent the cue from raising up out of there. And since we've already discussed the importance of a level cue in your stroke, you can see just how important a consideration that is. Few players achieve the level of concentration and relaxation necessary to shoot the majority of shots this way. But it's still the best beginner's bridge there is, because it's at once simple and efficient, and I think as you progress you'll find a welcome spot for this bridge in your game.

Picture 6 shows you pool's basic bridge for advanced play. There are all kinds of subtle variations on it, depending on what's comfortable for your hand and efficient for your stroke. But basically it's the same as the last bridge except that you form a loop with your thumb and index finger. Ideally, your thumb and finger will come together at the tips, as though you were pinching something (keep your mind on pool, please); but it's possible that you may create

Picture 6.

a bridge which feels more firm and comfortable to you by placing the index finger *inside* the thumb, so that the pad of the thumb contacts the edge of the fingernail. But do *not* form a bridge in which the finger rests *outside* the thumb; that won't serve you well at all.

However you form it, that loop will also be in contact with your middle finger, at about the second joint. Many master players have taught that the middle finger should be folded so as to rest nail-down on the table; the points of contact between hand and table then become the ring and little fingers and most of the thumb. The three-point distribution of balance led to the name *tripod* bridge. I'm more comfortable spreading the middle finger out myself, and I think the vast majority of today's players are, too. You'll then have these points of contact between hand and table: heel of hand, three fingertips, base, and maybe even tip of thumb.

There are four factors involved in the choice of bridge you form for any given shot; you provide two of those, the game provides the other two. The two factors that control your decision are what feels best and what works best for you. What the game dictates is (1) how much room you have in which to place your bridge hand down; and (2) what part of the cue ball you wish to strike. And naturally, any single shot may involve those latter factors singly or simultaneously. So let's take a look at some of the practical variations.

Either of the two bridges we've discussed thus far are fine for striking the cue ball at its center or points lower than that. In fact, you could use the bridge of Picture 6 to strike the cue ball above its center with no problem at all, just by retracting your last three fingers slightly; that would automatically elevate your loop and thus the cue. But the catch is that you may not always be able to place your entire hand on the table, and Picture 7 shows you what to do for

Picture 7.

a reliable bridge when space is at a premium. Your thumb and first two fingers stay in the same relationship; all you do is raise up on your three fingertips. Obviously this bridge lends itself well to shots where you want to strike the cue ball above center; situations will also arise where you must both use a bridge like this and strike the cue ball low, and you'll have to be careful in those spots because the plane of your stroke will be *down at* the cue ball, rather than through it levelly.

That can be done, of course, and generally the above three bridges are the ones that correspond to positive situations on the table for you. The following bridges correspond to cue-ball situations that can make you swallow hard first: over another object ball(s), and near or on a rail.

When you must address the cue ball from over another object ball, you can forget about any kind of loop between your thumb and index finger, and for a super reason: if you did that, you'd be hiding the tip of your cue from sight. So it's got to be as you see in Picture 8. Your hand stands on

Picture 8.

the last three fingertips (assuming you have room to put that many down; you may occasionally have to accomplish this with two). Your index finger is doubled under (otherwise you'd be poking the ball immediately underneath, and besides your bridge is firmer this way). Your thumb meets the second joint of your index finger, and your cue rides over that ridge. It almost sounds heroic, but actually an over-the-ball situation like this is nothing you want to see. Still, such situations come up.

When the cue ball comes to rest near to or frozen (touching) on a cushion (and the difference between those two circumstances is significant enough that each requires a bridge of its own), you've got your choice of several bridges. Which one you employ is largely a matter of the angle at which you want to shoot.

For instance, if you have the luxury of a few inches between cue ball and rail, you may form modified versions of the bridges we've already discussed with your hand on the rail rather than the table (Pictures 9, 10, 11). I say "modified" because the rail position automatically elevates your bridge over the base of the cue ball, making levelness impossible, and your normal bridge would raise the cue even higher than that. So the three bridges you see here are all flattened-down versions of their former selves. (In your early learning stages, don't worry too much about the bridge of Picture 11; it comes up in those rare and unwelcome situations in which, despite the disadvantageous cue-ball position, you still need to *drive* it someplace for your next shot.)

But now if you face that same angle from a frozen-or-damn-close-to-frozen cue-ball position, the bridge of Picture 11 becomes something of a spearfishing proposition, as you see in Picture 12. You can't use your conventional index finger–thumb loop bridge at all, because you'd hide both your cue tip and what's left to see of the cue ball. The closest you can come to achieving that sort of bridge is

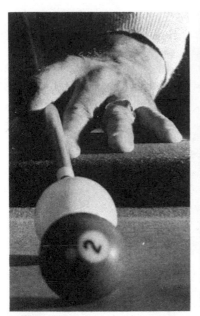

Picture 9.

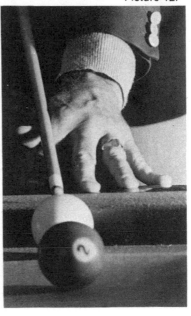

Picture 10.

Picture 11.

Picture 12.

what you see in Picture 13; the cue gets cradled between thumb and forefinger, all right, but it's an unsteady bridge for most players. What's better is the bridge of Picture 14. It's a simple, nearly flat-handed affair in which you aim by guiding the cue along the side of your index finger, much as an archer guides his arrow. Keep the thumb close enough in so that there is gentle but firm contact between both thumb and finger and the cue tip; too loose *or* too firm a bridge will defeat your purpose.

For some reason, it's the shots which require shooting away from (or, for purists, perpendicular to) the rail that

Picture 13.   Picture 14.

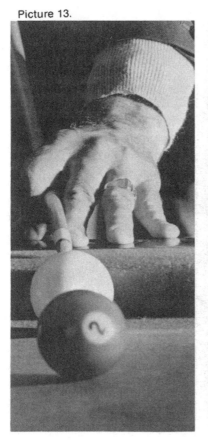

intimidate players most. Shooting off a rail is seldom much of a bargain in any form, but the bridges we've discussed so far have always felt more firm and comfortable to beginners than the ones coming up. Those are the bridges required by shots that *parallel* the rail (or come close to doing that). And paradoxically, although these bridges are somewhat more awkward to learn and form, the shots involved are generally shallow-angle and not all that difficult; the last three bridges, by contrast, are easy to learn but tough to get confident about, and will be called upon for some of your game's very roughest spots.

Picture 15 shows you what I mean. What the thumb does here is get the hell out of the way, tucked into the palm. The index finger crosses over and pins the cue against the rail. Note that this is what a right-handed player does to address a shot along the rail on his *left*; when the shot occurs over on his right, I advocate an open-thumb bridge as long as there's room to get your bridge hand down, as in Picture 16. If the shot offers you a sharper angle than par-

Picture 15.

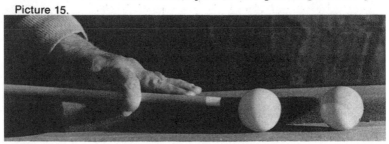

Picture 16.

allel or close to parallel to the rail, as in Picture 17, you can't go open-thumb because your body must turn and you don't have room to bridge on the table any more. The bridge of Picture 17 (and an alternate version in Picture 18) is applicable to either the left-hand or right-hand rail. The awkwardness of all these shots comes up because in order

Picture 17.

Picture 18.

to keep your cue level (a rule you simply must observe if you're going to play the game right), you have to slide more of the cue over the rail itself, and it's hard to get used to that with the same fluidity you'd have elsewhere. *(You'll do it, but not everyone can.)*

So much for inertia. Let's talk about hitting the ball.

The ideal pool stroke is more simple than you'd believe. The thing is, it's so simple that almost no one can do it. I know that sounds contradictory, but what happens is that most players—well above 90 percent—cannot resist the temptation to add something extra to that simple little stroke.

More specifically, very few players are able to limit the action of their strokes to *the movement of the forearm and wrist.* When nothing above the elbow moves, that's the essence of the perfect pool stroke, called a *pendulum* stroke by the classicists because the lower arm simulates the action of the pendulum of a grandfather clock. And believe it or not, that's enough physical activity to accomplish all but a handful of practical pool shots.

Where most pool players go astray is in first learning pool games that require the balls to be broken wide open to begin the game, as in Eight-Ball or Nine-Ball. Rare indeed is the player who can accomplish that break effectively without getting some upper-arm movement (and, frequently, most of his body) into the act. And since breaking the balls is the first thing most players learn to do, they never come quite all the way back to gentleness.

You've got an edge here. You're just learning, with a minimum of bad habits to break. If you can learn pool with a correct stroke from the beginning, you'll learn it scads faster. That's why I emphasize the importance of fundamentals: the best pool players simply practice the best fundamentals with the fewest embellishments. And you have a chance to achieve those same fundamentals in far less time than it will take you to reach their level. You can be sure that achieving their level *without* good fundamentals will be an upstream swim all the way.

Check this out for yourself. Assume your regular, comfortable stance, take a few practice strokes, and turn your head so you can see your elbow while stroking. See all that movement back there? Now concentrate on forearm movement only. Keep your eye on your elbow if you have to, but quiet that upper arm down. Once you get the feel of it, turn your head back to normal shooting position, but don't stop stroking. Now *that's* what the ultimate pool stroke is all about.

It's theoretically available for everyone to learn, but since many people never do, there's a chance you may not get *quite* all the way there either. *Some* upper-arm movement will be all right, as long as you apply yourself to the game seriously and always try to keep that movement minimal. But as long as you're just learning pool now, you might as well try to get the most ideal start you can.

Let's talk a little about the primary hitee, the cue ball, to which you'll apply all this delicacy. You're going to have to buddy up to that ball if you expect to play pool even passably. It can equally be your best friend or your worst enemy in the game, and the better you get to know it, the more you'll understand why it's all white. The cue ball is *purity,* friends, because that's where you'll find every secret the entire game has to offer. You wouldn't *believe* what a good player can make the white ball do.

Now then: if you subscribe to the theory of first-we-crawl-then-we-walk, and that's the progression most of us do go through, then you surely ought to go for this one. I'm going to propose that you begin to learn this marvelous game in the total absence of object balls. Just you and the cue ball, to start with, and a sequence of exercises for you to accomplish before you ever begin playing any kind of pool game. It will take you some extra days of practice, test your patience, and may even draw a giggle or two if you play in commercial rooms. Let them laugh. (And take their names. We'll get those guys.)

But here's why this disciplined learning of the cue ball is so worthwhile: while the fundamental object of pool is to put an object ball in the pocket, you'll find that to be of minimal value in and of itself—*unless* you can put the cue ball somewhere advantageous at the same time. (Which, of course, can be as simple as merely stopping it dead.) So getting acquainted with the cue ball in a vacuum is not only logical; it's practical. You'll begin to learn the game with a consistent stroke and a measure of cue-ball control. and thus learn the fundamentals of pocketing *and* position almost at the same time. That will put you eons ahead of other students of the game right there, and your learning from that point on will be accelerated as well. Any expert will tell you that the cue ball is very nearly the whole game.

The next sequence of diagrams looks like a primer in Boy Scout signals, but actually it represents the various cue-ball options available to you on different shots.

In Diagrams 3 through 11, eight of the nine diagrams show you a type of cue-ball hit other than dead center. And in seven of those eight cases, I can earnestly recommend that you stray

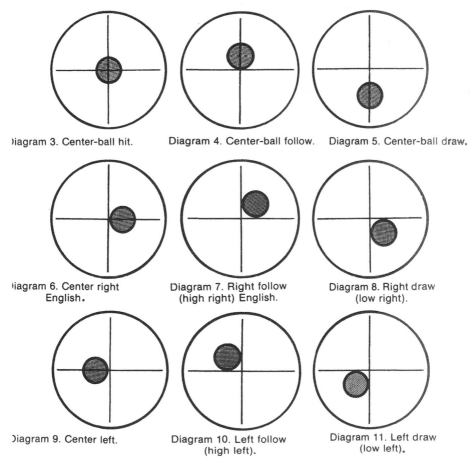

Diagram 3. Center-ball hit.   Diagram 4. Center-ball follow.   Diagram 5. Center-ball draw.

Diagram 6. Center right
English.

Diagram 7. Right follow
(high right) English.

Diagram 8. Right draw
(low right).

Diagram 9. Center left.

Diagram 10. Left follow
(high left).

Diagram 11. Left draw
(low left).

no farther from the center of the cue ball than the width of your cue tip, especially while learning. The lone exception is Diagram 5, center-ball draw, in which case you should attempt to cue the ball as low as you safely can (but remember, you've got to keep your cue level, otherwise you're going to be launching the cue ball). The key word here is "safely." Not only can the various forms of English (vertical spin) be accomplished by going just outside the ball's center, but the farther toward the edge of the ball you go, the less actual contact area there is, and you're begging for a costly miscue

What a cue ball can be made to do on any given shot can be generalized this way:

1. It can stop in its tracks. Obviously, what you need in order to accomplish this is a shot where cue ball and object ball line up straight for the hole. But there'll be plenty of those, and expert players can even stop the cue ball in its tracks on shots with a few degrees of angle to them.

2. It can follow in the general direction of the object ball.

3. It can come back in the general direction of the shooter, commonly referred to as "draw."

4. It can deflect to either side. These are an effect of the game's "cut" shots, or shots in which cue ball, object ball, and pocket form a visible angle. They're quite negotiable, but generally less preferable than straight shots because you can't predict the cue ball's future with the same accuracy. You may occasionally hear the phrase "cut the ball backwards," but that's something of a misnomer. It's possible to cut an object ball slightly in excess of 90°, though.

You might also note that I don't distinguish between cut shots to the left and those to the right. Theoretically, there's no reason to; yet the vast majority of all players, well over 90 percent, feel in their hearts of hearts that they prefer cutting a ball one way to cutting it the other. None of that for us. Lay down your prejudices.

The cue ball hits in Diagrams 3 through 11, of course, all

come into play in order to achieve beneficial follow, draw, and cut-shot action, and advanced players will frequently have their *choice* of cue-ball hits to accomplish the same thing. But, as you're learning the game, let me give you a tip, one that you cannot possibly learn too well. *Wherever possible, stay in the middle of the cue ball.* Whether it's stop, follow, or draw that you want, do it by stroking center, above center, or low center, respectively. Center-ball play can accomplish an astonishing majority of pool shot and position requirements. And if you're willing to forget for a moment that this is a beginner's book, center-ball play is a common denominator (and one of the best secrets) of the top 15 or 20 players in the world.

Why make such a fuss about this, when it sounds so simple? Because English, once learned, is an incredible temptation to pool players. Somehow or other, it gets into their heads that nothing much will happen unless the cue ball is made to spin. That's a trap that most intermediate players fall into at one time or another, most of them for good. Avoid it.

English is not a total villain in the game, of course. It's the incorrect application of English that does players in; the erring player will either use English where none was needed, or use more of it than he should have. *The correct use of English in pool is to create an angle of travel for the cue ball that the shot does not make available as it lies,* and the best strokes always involve the most moderate English. It would be awfully nice for you to have both. So let's get stroking.

Diagram 12 shows you how to begin. Take a position facing the opposite long rail, place the cue ball far enough off the rail that you can bridge comfortably, and draw an imaginary line between the facing diamonds on the rail (those diamonds, by the way, are functional, not decorative). Now see how close you can come to stroking the cue ball, with a dead center hit (Diagram 3), so it travels to-

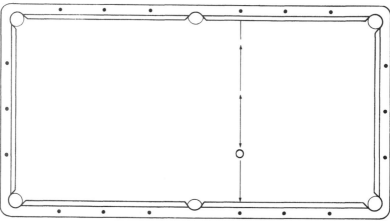

Diagram 12.

ward the diamond facing you and then back to you. Use the diamonds to check the straightness of your delivery.

You'll find this to be less simple than it sounds, at least for the first several tries, so let's review the checklist of stroke fundamentals:

1. Take a comfortable stance, with your weight evenly balanced.

2. Keep your head and bridge hand perfectly steady.

3. Keep the cue level.

4. Hold the cue in your fingers, not your palm.

5. Use a compact, smooth, soft stroke, limited to lower arm as much as possible.

Don't worry about speed; your stroke will add power automatically as you get used to it. You don't have to hit the cue ball very hard to accomplish this exercise, and there's no reason yet for you to try hitting it any harder than you have to.

As this simple stroke begins to feel comfortable to you, and you can see some improvement in what you're doing, add some practice strokes to the routine. These are the equivalent of what you see a batter do in the batter's box while waiting for the pitch, or what a golfer does before putting. The idea of these is to approximate the speed of the stroke you'll actually use, and to get the feel of the shot before you hit it. Three to five such practice strokes will do fine; while learning, try to make it the same number each time.

Now try the same thing using the hits of Diagrams 4 and 5. The path of cue-ball travel should still be the same, but I think you'll begin to feel a difference in each of the three hits. When applying draw (Diagram 5), you may want to add a smidgen of speed in order to underspin the ball with authority.

I'll grant you that this is not a wildly exciting exercise; in return for that, I'm not going to ask you to do it very long. If you can simply relax and be a little patient, a competent cue-ball stroke should come to you within minutes. A few minutes' practice, just for the first few days in which you spend any time at the game, is not all that great a penance, and it will certainly start you on the way to pool heaven.

The next stage of this drill is to try it the *length* of the table, rather than its width (Diagram 13). Pool tables are, or should be, marked with spots at the head and foot of the playing surface, to facilitate the correct racking of the balls.

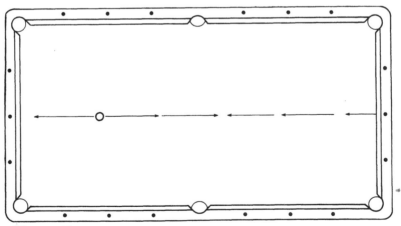

Diagram 13.

Place the cue ball behind either spot, and aim at the other spot, with enough speed to bring the cue ball back to you. If your center-ball hit and stroke are true, the cue ball should return over the spot you began with. This will be tricky for you (although old-timers used to teach this by making the student stroke the ball between two coins a quarter inch apart, and it required nothing less than perfection to pass those coins *both* ways without touching them. I'm not that old-fashioned, or sadistic, for that matter). But you'll get it.

Once you've demonstrated your ability to stroke the ball in a straight line, go on to the hits of Diagrams 6 through 11. Don't fix any targets this time; I just want you to see and feel the effects of the various hits as the ball engages a cushion. Then we'll go on to something a little more advanced.

Place the cue ball as you see in Diagram 14, far enough in front of the right-hand corner pocket that you can bridge comfortably. This time, aim at that third diamond just

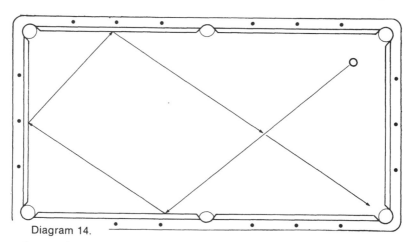

Diagram 14.

above the opposite side pocket (I told you those diamonds were useful) with a center-ball hit, and see if you can drive the ball off three rails into the opposite corner pocket. I've given you the correct angle; your correct cue-ball hit and stroke should do the rest. It's also a good chance for you to see how little force you actually need to drive the ball around the table.

You'll get this down in a matter of minutes, too. The catch is, when you move up to trying this shot with either follow or draw English, you'll find that the results are no longer the same. Even when you stay in the middle of the cue ball, as you should, center follow or center draw will alter the angles of a shot *considerably*. (The reason that didn't happen in the first drills is that you were attempting a straight line, with no angle involved.) In order to pocket the cue ball using either follow or draw, you're going to have to adjust your point of aim either down or up the rail, respectively. How much you adjust depends upon your precise hit, stroke, and speed (the last affects angles, too; like I said, this is some game).

Once you get the feel of this, go on to the hits of Diagrams 6, 7, and 8; once again, you'll find that you must adjust your aim in each case. Then switch pockets and shoot the exercise in the opposite direction, using the left-hand English hits in Diagrams 9, 10, and 11. Don't worry about how many times you can do this in a row; that's unimportant at first and simpler than you'd believe once learned. All we're trying to achieve here is to get you comfortable with your new stroke by testing it with simple, purposeful tasks.

Bear with me and discipline yourself through this simple routine for your first few days of pool. Just a few minutes a day is all it takes. You'll be glad you did once we take on the *object* balls, and they loom large ahead even as we speak.

4

Pocketing

Putting a ball in a hole, of course, is what pool is ultimately all about. If you never did anything else but put an object ball in a pocket each time you shot, you could ascend to the game's throne at once. You can't do that, of course; not only will shots become unavailable to you throughout the game, but even if shots were available to infinity, human error would catch up to you in no time and set you down. So in the metaphorical sense, the game always wins; nobody pockets balls endlessly.

With that as a given, let's try and get you making a majority of the shots you should. It won't come overnight. How long it does take to make you a proficient shotmaker has much to do with your eyes—not just vision, but your spatial-relationship aptitudes—and your own gifts for hand-eye coordination. But I can teach you some excellent habits.

The first of these habits is to bring that same sweet stroke you're working on now to the art of pocketing object balls. I know that sounds almost too simple to mention, but it's not. How many times have you seen a weekend tennis player slap backhands down the line and into the corners during practice, only to run around the stroke completely once the set begins? Same process. There's no getting around this: pool shots intimidate pool players, and not just at the beginner level of the game. Naturally, beginners are vulnerable to fear of a lot more shots than those more advanced at the game.

And the very antidote you'd want for that is confidence. That's why I've advised you to learn your stroke in the absence of object balls. You're free to bring a stroke you're already familiar and comfortable with to shotmaking, and that's where confidence begins. Let's take on a few rudimentary shots, and I want you to stroke them the exact same way you did when you were hitting the cue ball only.

Let's begin with a look at shotmaking theory. When two spheres touch, such as when cue ball meets object ball, the actual point of contact is just about microscopic. I have two good reasons for reminding you of this. One is to cleanse you of the temptation to aim a pool shot by looking for that little pinpoint on the object ball. Forget about that. Steve Austin couldn't pick it out, not even with a second bionic eye. That's the incorrect way to aim, even though you may think that's what you're doing. (Interestingly, I can lead you to some dynamite players who will tell you, in all sincerity, that they really don't quite know what it is they're aiming at. Actually, they do, but not at the conscious level. They execute successfully anyway, but we'll talk about the specifics of aiming, you and I, on the premise that knowledge cannot possibly hurt you.)

The second thing to remember about that point of aim is that although it's awesomely small, at least it's the same size on just about all pool shots. (The exception to this is the thinnest cut shots of the game, those approaching 90 degrees, where you really have to try and cut that last coat of paint off the ball. In those rare cases, you actually must hit less of the object ball than on less challenging shots.

We'll let that go for now.) On a shot where cue ball and object ball and pocket form a straight line, your point of aim is exactly the same size as it is on shots where you must cut the ball sharply in either direction. It's simply less visible to you in the latter case. Thus the term "hard shot" is really something of a misnomer in pool; it's more a matter of having less frontal view of the point of aim. That's not harder; it's just different. Learn to think of pool shots in this positive way. It will do wonders for your attitude, and eventually you'll learn how highly mental a game pool is. Attitude can make a 180-degree turnaround in your pool game.

So how *do* you aim a pool shot? I thought you'd never ask. Have a look at Diagram 15, a simple, perfectly straight shot into a side pocket (we'll start with a side pocket shot

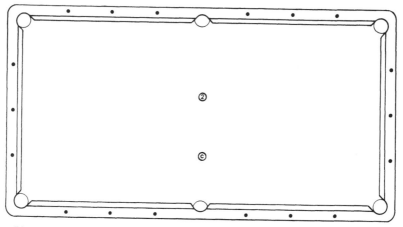

Diagram 15. The correct way to aim a shot like this . . .

because those are the widest pockets on the table). Even if you've never played pool before, it should be obvious that you wouldn't need a telescopic infrared viewfinder for a shot like this; you'd immediately recognize that to pocket the object ball, you'd only have to advance the cue ball in a straight line toward it.

Set yourself up with a shot like this, assume your comfortable shooting stance, and before you fire, rehearse the shot in your mind. See the cue ball stopping dead in its tracks—you're to hit this shot with center ball at first—and the object ball rolling obediently holeward. Then do it. If it's possible, I recommend that you try a shot like this before you read the next paragraph. Once you've made this shot, it will become much easier to explain to you exactly what you did.

Did you get the thing into the pocket yet? (Or, as they used to say in the Army, are you getting ahead of the instructor?) Well, in either case, if you have success with a pool shot—this one or any other—it's because you stopped looking at the shot as shown in Diagram 15 and advanced yourself to the vision of Diagram 16. You saw the correct

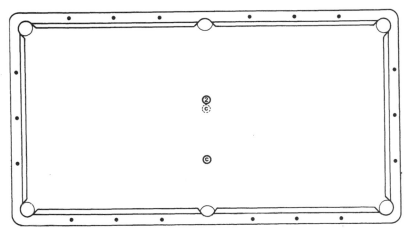

Diagram 16. . . . is to see it like this.

juxtaposition of cue ball and object ball *at the point of contact* that was necessary to pocket the ball. That's why I propose you mentally rehearse every shot before shooting; it lets you see exactly where the cue ball must go to achieve success. And that's far preferable to squinting after a little germ-size area on the naked object ball.

Beginners are generally taught to begin aiming by drawing an imaginary line between the pocket and the object ball you want to sink. Generally, you do this with the aid of your cue; you point at that line you see with your cue, as though you were going to drive the object ball home without using the cue ball. That's a valid learning technique for beginners, but many of them mistake it for the entire aiming process. What happens then is that the player spends the rest of his playing days trying to see pinpoints because he was taught to find a point on the ball originally. Do yourself a favor and try visualizing correct placement of the cue ball instead. Seeing a 2¼ inch diameter ball is considerably easier than seeing a pinpoint.

All right. If you can pocket the shot of Diagram 15 with some consistency, branch out a bit and set up other straight-in shots for yourself. Then try them using the cue-ball hits of Diagrams 4 and 5, follow and draw English, respectively. (Remember to be gentle when using follow; you hardly want to send the cue ball into the subway after its quarry.) You'll want to be firmer than that when using draw because the cue ball must be made to underspin (in other words, move towards you) all the way to the object ball if you want it to come back to you after contact. If this puzzles you, think of a foul-tipped baseball; it doesn't move backward until it touches the ground and its spin can take effect.

Before we move on to the next stage of shotmaking, let me give you the best demonstration you could ask for of why you've been counseled not to use English unless you simply must. Try the simple, straight-in shot of your choice using any of the hits in Diagrams 6 through 11, and see what happens. Fun, huh? The damn thing isn't straight any more. If you achieve a perfectly straight-on hit with English on the cue ball, the object ball will *not* continue in a straight line. Right-hand English (draw more so than follow) will throw the object ball off to the left, and vice versa. To some degree, the balls act as gears do; spin on one will create some opposite spin on the other. The balls don't care if you meant to apply English or not. They only do what you direct them to. So not only must you concentrate on center-ball play, you also must take care to hit the precise point on the *cue* ball that you aim at. Uncontrolled English, intentional or not, will do you in almost without fail.

Naturally, there's more at stake in this innocuous exercise than the mere pocketing of a ball. You should be acquainting yourself with the happy little mental process of sizing up a shot correctly and mentally rehearsing the successful completion of the shot. That's something that should accompany every single pool shot you ever try, even the most elementary ones. Simple shots are still quite missable, as you've probably already learned.

As you show progress at this, try setting up straight shots of greater length. Do this gradually, as you would anything else. Straight-in shots constitute a minority of the shots in a pool game simply because a player who's able to leave himself a sequence of straight shots is an expert, and there aren't all that many experts. Straight shots are what you ultimately hope to reduce your pool game *to,* but it's time for you to learn to cut a ball.

Remember, it theoretically makes no difference whether the angle of a cut shot is narrow or wide (unless you insist on setting yourself up with something really heathenish). The area of contact between cue ball and object ball does not vary in size, only in frontal visibility, and you therefore aim all your cut shots the same way: by *seeing* the cue ball in correct contact with the object ball, just as you did with the straight-ins. Diagrams 17, 18, and 19 review the process for you. Draw an imaginary line between the pocket and the center of the object ball; in fact, don't be embarrassed about making this aim physically with your cue. All the best players still do it now and then. Once you've got your

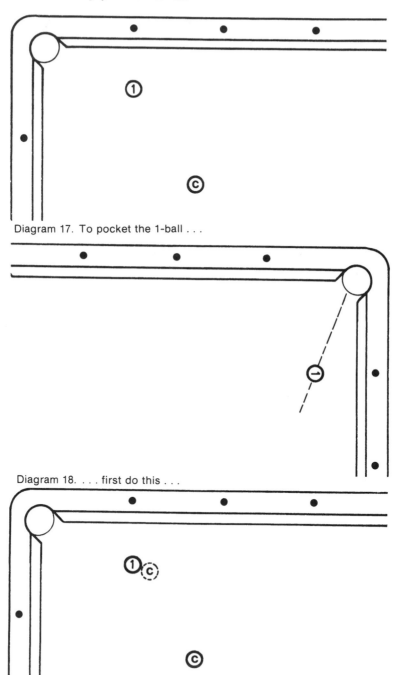

Diagram 17. To pocket the 1-ball . . .

Diagram 18. . . . first do this . . .

Diagram 19. . . . then see it like this.

point of aim, get back behind the cue ball and *project* it into correct scoring contact. Rehearse the correct execution of the shot mentally. Then do it.

The vast majority of cut shots will also involve the cue ball's meeting one or more rails. Since successful pool playing has to do with the *consecutive* pocketing of balls, it's not too early to get you thinking about the speed of the cue ball coming off the rail(s). All pool boils down to pocketing an object ball *and* putting the cue ball someplace advantageous. Those two objectives are a matched set. One is worthless without the other.

Accordingly, the next phase of practice for your cut shots should involve the sinking of one object ball plus correct cue-ball position for another. Don't rush into this; spend some time learning to cut in one practice ball at a time. Start with shots you're comfortable with and gradually increase the angles until you can really slice the thing fairly thin.

But once you feel the guesswork going out of your shot-making, and you at least understand the *mechanics* of shot-making even if your actual shots aren't all falling, start the drill of Diagram 20. The idea is to pocket the 1-ball and

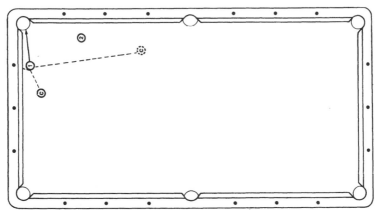

Diagram 20. Looks simple, and it is, but actually it's the basis for all championship play.

bring the cue ball out far enough—but not too far—to have a good shot on the 2-ball. When you get familiar with that, place the 2-ball anywhere else on the table you wish, then do what you have to do for a reasonable shot on it at the same time you make the 1-ball. The shot of Diagram 20 can and should be accomplished with a center-ball hit on the cue ball; you might wish to graduate to cut shots and second-ball position play using other hits on the cue ball. Don't worry about covering in your practice all the conceivable situations the game will ever hand you; you can't possibly. The objective is to learn what can be done with the cue ball, just as it was when we were practicing without any object balls.

Again, it's recommended that you stay with center hits on the cue ball, whether center, follow, or draw. If you do want to experiment with English, remember that spin on the cue ball affects the flight of the object ball. So if you wanted to cut a ball to your left, using right-hand English, you'd have to compensate for the English by hitting the object slightly fuller than you'd sight for using center ball. The right-hand English will "throw" the object ball slightly to the left. How much actual compensating you do has mostly to do with cue-ball speed; the less speed, the more "throw," and vice versa. Also, draw English has a greater "throw" effect than either follow or center.

It might seem like we're going through all this rather quickly, but the fact is that that's all there is. All the shots of pool can be categorized as either straight-in or cut shots. You can set up practice shots for yourself until Armageddon, but you'd do nothing to whet your competitive instinct and you'd probably get very bored in the bargain. Accomplishing stroke, cue-ball control, and some shotmaking ability might take you a few extra weeks' worth of practice time (and I'm not saying that's all it takes to make a *player* out of you, but just what it takes to get the basics down); but I think you'll progress faster if you take your practice accomplishments into reasonable competition. Try to find an opponent of your speed or maybe slightly better, and make it a point of every practice session not merely to execute the exercises but to *learn* from them, too. Be patient, and when playing competitively, always strive to play as correctly as your practice has taught you. Don't let the pressure of winning or losing tempt you into changing your fundamentals. It happens all the time, and not just in pool either. Believe in what you're doing and take *consistency* to the table with you.

I haven't given you any alternate two-ball drills to go with Diagram 20 simply because there are an infinite number of them. It does make sense for you to assign yourself drills in which you must run the gamut of center, follow, and draw for correct position. I'll give you three practice drills for multiple object balls now, and when you can master all these, you'll be reading the wrong book. These are no cinches.

The objective of the drill in Diagram 21 is to pocket all four balls in the side pockets—which ball goes where makes no difference—without driving the cue ball to a rail. You

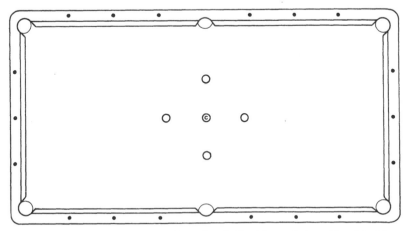

Diagram 21. Make all four balls, using both side pockets, without sending the cue ball to the rail.

can place the cue ball anywhere you want, inside the diamond or not, to begin. This is an ancient hustlers' trick,
and the secret is to leave yourself a very slight angle on
each ball as you play position. If you get straight-in on a
ball anywhere along the way, you're dead. This will test
your ability to shoot softly.

Diagram 22 shows you another sort of challenge. Make a
circle of all 15 object balls, start anywhere inside the circle
that you like, and pocket the balls, in any pocket you wish,
without leaving the circle or touching a second ball while
scoring the first. Obviously you can't use follow English
and stay within the circle; that leaves stop-ball and draw,
and this drill will enhance your capacity for both.

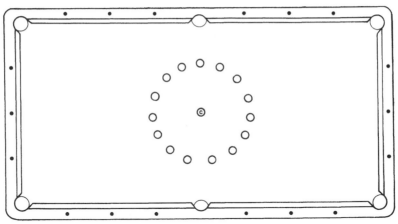

Diagram 22. Shoot 'em off, anywhere you like. But *don't* leave the circle,
and don't touch a second object ball.

Diagram 23 is the hardest of all. This time, you're to
pocket as many balls *in order* as you can, starting with the
ball nearest the middle of the bottom rail. You're allowed
to employ the rails this time; the sequence is negotiable
without ever driving the cue ball to a rail, but it takes a
player of pretty-near-national class to do it. Again, you
don't use follow English, and it should also be apparent

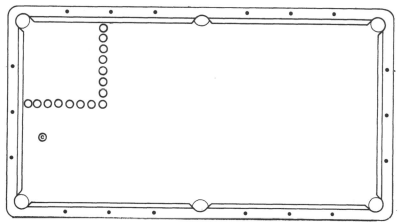

Diagram 23. Make these balls in order in Pocket X, without touching a second ball.

that you don't use stop-ball either. It's all a matter of center-ball hits or draw, depending on which side of the object ball the cue ball winds up on; and again, you must leave yourself some angle on each ball. You may use one rail or two to get position; one is better.

Banks, caroms, and other puzzlements

Suppose there's no open path between cue ball and object ball and pocket. Object balls are loose, but you see no open chances to readily knock any of them in; it's water, water everywhere, but not a drop to drink, right? Well, yes and no. Balls are available for you to make *indirectly* in a higher percentage of situations than you think if you know where and how to look for them. I'm not saying you should play recklessly and go for the most remote mind-bending miracle shots that you see; quite the contrary. "Hidden" shots such as the ones we're about to discuss are frequently quite simple to make; in their difficult, low-probability stages, they're to be avoided except by experts, maybe even then. And of course you don't choose these kinds of shots in preference to open shots, unless the open shot in question is unattractive to you and the two-ball or bank shot in question is something of a cinch.

Let's start with bank shots since they involve only a single object ball. For those of you who have a grounding in high school geometry, bank shots are by and large a matter of bisecting angles.

For instance, Diagram 24 shows you a natural bank shot, which can be pocketed by a center-ball, straight-on hit, just

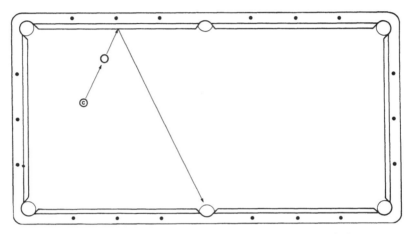

Diagram 24. This bank shot is no harder than a straight-in shot.

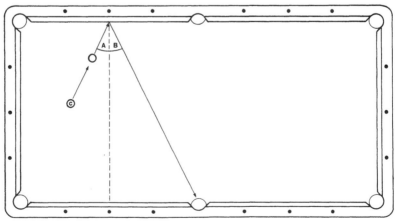

Diagram 25. Here's why—perfectly matched angles A & B.

as though it were lined up straight for a hole someplace. It's natural because the angle between cue ball and object ball is identical to the angle between object ball and pocket. You can see that in Diagram 25. What you have to learn to do is draw that dotted line with your eyes. And they won't all lie as fat and juicy as this one.

The object ball in Diagram 26 lies where it did in the last two diagrams, but now the cue ball is parallel to it. How

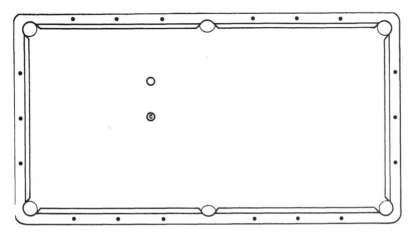

Diagram 26. This bank . . .

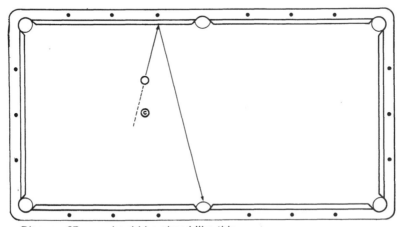

Diagram 27. : . . should be aimed like this . . .

do you aim now? By bisecting an angle, as in Diagram 27. That dotted line represents the hit you need on the object ball *to drive it to a point halfway between where it is now and that near side pocket.* Why halfway? Because we're aiming for that other side pocket, and that's the other half of the overall angle that you must cut in half precisely in order to make the shot.

You may find this point of aim tricky to determine at first, especially if the object ball is near or frozen to a rail. (Frozen balls are no picnic to bank for any level of player.) One way you might look at it, if the geometric language

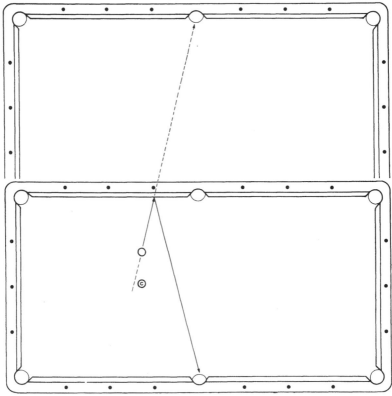

Diagram 28. . . . or even this, if you can visualize it this way.

doesn't seem practical to you, is to visualize another pool table smack up against the one you occupy (Diagram 28). If you aim the shot correctly for that far side-pocket mirage, you'll make it back in its real world.

You'll rarely see a player stroke a bank shot with anything but center draw. He stays in the center because, as we've seen already, English will alter the object ball's path (unless for some very advanced reasons he *needs* to do that); and he uses draw because, as we've seen already, what you do to the cue ball imparts the opposite to the object ball. Draw on the cue ball makes the object ball follow, which is its straightest and most natural roll. Bank shots can be made with high ball if there's simply no other way, but you can expect the object ball to behave somewhat less reliably.

Three of the game's other typical bank shots are shown in Diagrams 29, 30, and 31, and the next six diagrams (32-37) show you the two ways of aiming each. While you're learning the game, I think you'll do well to limit your bank shot attempts to the *short* banks, that is, those which see the object ball travel the width of the table, not the length. Leave the long banks for the experts.

Now let's see some of the possibilities involving a second object ball. The first and most obvious of these is the combination shot, in which you turn an object ball loose to act with your cue ball's power of attorney and knock a second ball into a hole.

It should be pretty clear that your chances of sinking a combination shot vary inversely with the distance between the object balls; the closer together the object balls are, the more attractive the shot becomes. Don't make that first object ball travel more than six inches to do its job, unless in emergencies or where the second ball is within a few inches of a pocket. If the two object balls you're considering are more than six inches apart, consider something else.

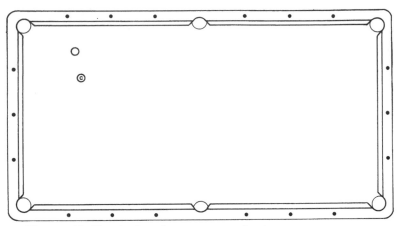

Diagram 29. The short-angle cross-corner bank.

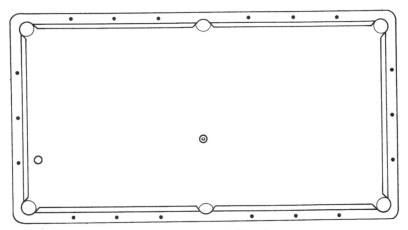

Diagram 30. The long, or "straight-back," bank.

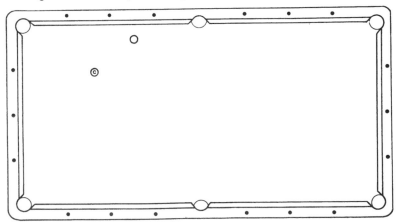

Diagram 31. The long cross-corner bank.

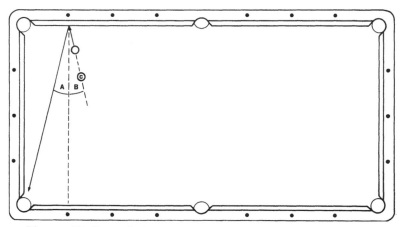

Diagram 32. One solution to Diagram 29.

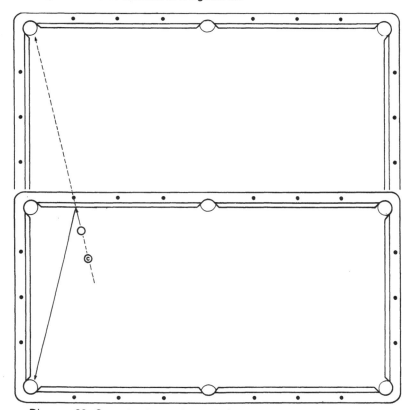

Diagram 33. Same bank, another solution.

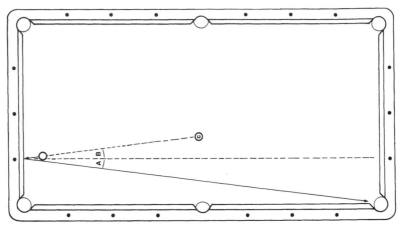

Diagram 34. The straight-back, seen correctly.

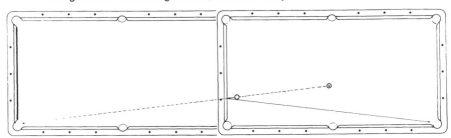

Diagram 35. Ditto.

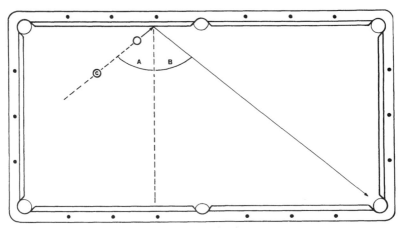

Diagram 36. The long cross-corner solved.

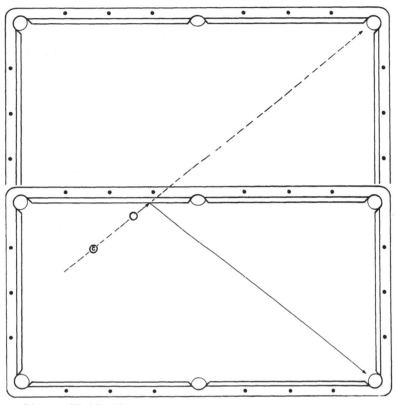

Diagram 37. Likewise.

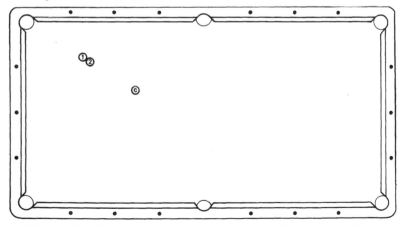

Diagram 38. The ideal combination shot, with object balls touching and in line.

Diagram 38 shows you the most elementary of combination shots, which offers you two frozen balls that line up perfectly for a pocket as they lie. The common terminology for this kind of shot is "on" or "dead," and if it's a disgruntled opponent pointing this out, either word will probably be followed by some sort of vituperation. Shots like this are actually tough to miss, because if you hit anywhere near the front of that first ball, the second one will go. (But they *can* be missed, and we're coming to that.) Don't be lazy when the game presents you with a gift like this; be a purist and aim on that first ball as carefully as though the second ball weren't there. Not only does it make the shot absolutely fail-safe, but your position play will benefit immensely. Believe me, you can't afford to let your concentration down *at all,* because if you do, the game will catch you napping every time.

Once the balls are any farther apart than a quarter inch (that's right, a quarter inch, and pool games are frequently won or lost by lots less than that), of course, it becomes mandatory to aim that first ball precisely. The shot of Diagram 39 is "on," but now it must be *made,* not merely struck. As long as the balls lie naturally, you need only aim correctly on the first ball to make the shot.

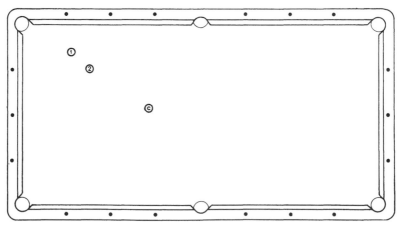

Diagram 39. Still makeable, but not the same shot . . .

But in the next stage of combination shot, Diagram 40, you'll have to aim *both* object balls because the shot does not lie naturally for the pocket at all. So it's a double aiming process. You draw a bead on the second object ball— the one you want to fall—to see where the first object ball must fit against it. Then you aim on the first object ball to see where you want the *cue* ball to fit to start the shot off correctly. It's all logical enough to explain, but off-angle combination shots like this fall into a category I call The Adam's Apple Gang. That's what usually bobs a little bit when these shots come up.

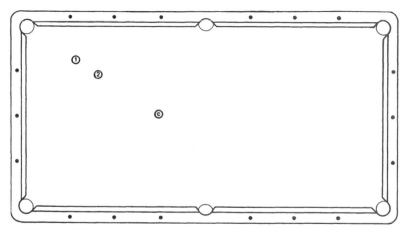

Diagram 40. . . . and still tougher.

Don't confuse these with the shot of Diagram 41, where balls which are both frozen and off-angle are presented for your shooting pleasure. I say "pleasure" because this shot is quite makable, even though it appears to be off. When two object balls are frozen (or, again, within a quarter inch of one another), you can use the first object ball to "throw" the second. And you accomplish that by doing the exact opposite of what you'd think: you strike the ball nearest you in Diagram 41 on its *left* side, and it will "throw" the second ball off to the right, holeward. (When the balls are spaced farther apart than that, you have to treat them as in Diagram 40. And if you suspect that the shots in which you can't quite tell whether the distance is or isn't a quarter inch are no fun, you've got it right.)

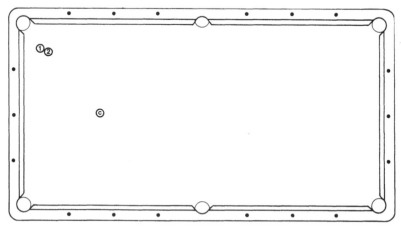

Diagram 41. Doesn't look good, but it is.

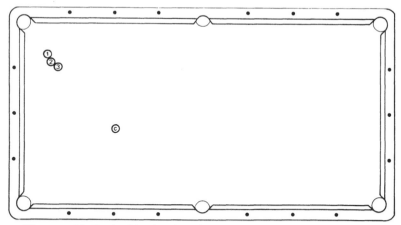

Diagram 42. So is this. In shots involving three or more balls, always read the third ball.

The same principle applies to three-ball shots like the one in Diagram 42 (but no more than three balls; when this shot occurs out of a cluster of more than three balls. it's the third one you gauge it from). You can see that the lie of the 1- and 2-balls points to the right of the corner pocket, a dim future indeed in pool terms. But you haven't given any thought yet to the lie of the 2- and *3*-balls, and that's important because the 3-ball occupies the correct position to throw the 2-ball to the left, and that will compensate for the lie of the 1-ball enough to pocket it. Now if the 3-ball were on the *left* side of the 2-ball, instead of the way you see it, the 1-ball could not possibly be made by hitting the 3-ball first. What you'd have to do in that case, if possible, would be to play the cue ball off the right side of the 2-ball to throw the 1-ball to the left and holeward; the 3-ball wouldn't figure in the shot at all.

Closely related to the combination shots, and other potential members of The Adam's Apple Gang, are the *kiss* shots. This aspect of the game isn't quite as pleasurable as it sounds, because accidental, unplanned "kisses" have been the difference between winning and losing scads of pool games. The term "kiss" refers to any contact between balls other than the one you create between cue ball and object ball.

Like the combination shots, kiss shots involve two object balls (once in a blue moon an expert will find a kiss shot involving three, but let's not worry about those now). The difference is that in a kiss shot, the object ball you strike with the cue ball is the ball to be sunk; it engages a second object ball along the way to complete the angle you need. And like the combinations, kiss shots can lie "dead" or they can lie so that you have to actively make them with your own skills.

Instead of aiming a kiss shot through the two object balls, as you do with combinations, you aim *between* them. Diagram 43 shows you just what you want to see in a kiss shot; the balls line up perfectly, and an imaginary line drawn between them would lead straight to the pocket. A center-ball hit on the cue ball, just about anywhere on the

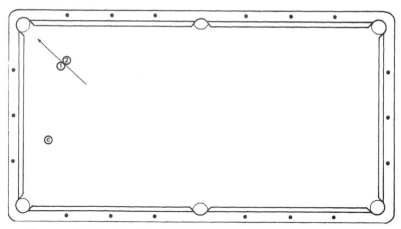

Diagram 43. The ideal kiss shot.

left side of the 1-ball, will make it glance off the 2-ball and into the pocket. Why a center-ball hit? Because of the "opposite-spin" effect we've already seen. If you put draw on the cue ball here, the 1-ball would *follow* through the 2-ball slightly instead of directly off it and would thus be headed to the right of the pocket. Follow on the cue ball would make the 1-ball *draw* slightly off the 2-ball, thus to the left of the pocket. (The same phenomena, of course, can

Diagram 44. Doesn't look good, but you can make the 1-ball with draw English.

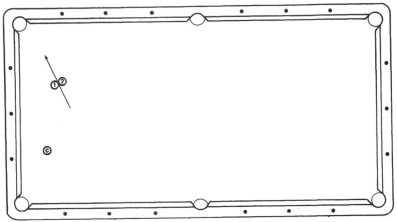

Diagram 45. Follow English here will make the 1-ball and draw off the 2-ball and in.

be used to successfully pocket kiss shots which do not lie true for the pocket. That's what we have in Diagrams 44 and 45, in which cases you'd use draw and follow, respectively.) And again, don't fool around with shots of more than a few inches between balls.

Carom shots are akin to kiss shots, except that the balls change roles. A carom involves the cue ball's rebounding off a first object ball in order to pocket a second one. You

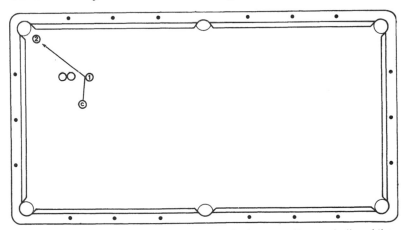

Diagram 46. A simple carom. You must aim between the cue ball and the 1-ball in order to get to the 2-ball correctly.

still aim between balls, as you did for kiss shots, but this time you aim between the cue ball and the first object ball to draw a bead on your target. Diagram 46 shows you an elementary carom, which is all I want you to concern yourself with for now. These shots are quite rare in Straight Pool, even as played by the best; where they come up a lot is in Rotation or its more popular variation, Nine-Ball, because those games offer a definite advantage in pocketing a ball other than the first one you strike. Carom shots are among the ringleaders of The Adam's Apple Gang as pool shots go, and are probably the very last sort of shot you should look for when stymied. Unless the object ball to be pocketed is very near a hold already, you're better off with a defensive play, or safety, than with a carom.

Naturally, for the imaginative, there are all sorts of exotic couplings of shots: combination-banks, combination-kisses, carom-kisses, and so on. Players who seek out these creative shots are the type that I would like to have on the proverbial slow boat, assuming pool could be played on one.

Those are all the legal ways I know to put an object ball in the pocket. All pocketable balls are either straight-in, cut shots, banks, kiss shots, combination shots, or caroms. There are techniques for *curving* the cue ball, especially that scourge of billiard-room proprietors, the massé shot; but they have no place in a beginner's book or, for that matter, a beginner's game. So now that you know the principles of shotmaking, let's learn some pool games to which you apply those principles.

5

Straight Pool

Straight Pool is the purist's delight. It's the predominant game of championship tournament play, although tournaments devoted to other games (pool's "short games") are gaining in popularity. It's the only pool game which involves transitions from one rack of balls to the next. Straight Pool has the potential, obviously, to keep a player at the table longer than in any other game; the other side of that coin is that the game can produce some of the slowest, dullest defensive matches imaginable. (Which is why all the other games are lumped into the category of "short games," especially by hustlers.) Whether Straight Pool—technically, 14.1 pocket billiards, for a reason we'll get to shortly—is the most *challenging* of all pool games, for all its majesty, depends largely upon whom you ask for an opinion.

I do feel that Straight Pool deserves the lion's share of attention in a book like this or in any other responsible form of pool instruction, because its principles for correct play ultimately not only govern but will actually improve your play in other games. That can be proved geographically: Straight Pool is a real stepchild in the South, even though pool itself is extremely popular there and always has been. Southern players are weaned on Nine-Ball (and occasionally Eight-Ball, too); and rare indeed is the Nine-Ball player who can make the adjustment to topflight Straight Pool. At the same time, the world's best Straight Pool is unarguably played along the East Coast; and *those* players have no trouble converting into wicked short-games players, too. With the exception of the great Luther "Wimpy" Lassiter, Southern sharks who invade New York and New Jersey are generally making collect calls home in short order.

So even if you do enjoy other forms of pool than Straight Pool, you'll be doing yourself a favor to learn Straight Pool as well as you can anyway. Sooner or later, you'll be drawing on every single one of its aspects. No other game puts it all together quite as well.

The essence of Straight Pool play is simple enough (in words, anyway): it's the ability to pocket a designated object ball *and*, on the same shot, send your cue ball into secondary clustered object balls to break them apart. That's how you achieve the transitions from rack to rack that we talked about; in this game, you re-rack the object balls when one is left open, so you have a rack of 14 balls and one in the clear, hence the name 14.1. And additionally, you will generally be called upon to apply break shots *within* each rack, multiple times, as well as between racks. Whether the cluster to be dealt with consists of 14 balls or just two, the principle remains the same.

If you could master the shot of Diagram 47—not just the mere pocketing of the 1-ball, but the consistent making available of loosened object balls for subsequent shots—you'd already know a great deal about break shots in general. Obviously this isn't the only break shot in the game, but it is an ideal one for several reasons. Diagrams 48 through 52 show you other of the common and practical break shots of the game. What I want you to recognize

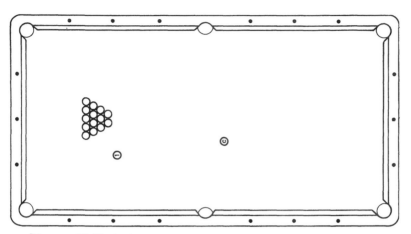

Diagram 47. Typical—and ideal—break shot.

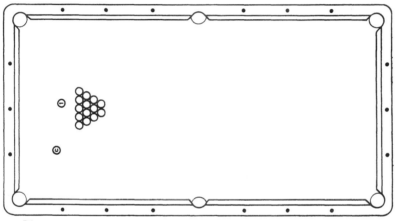

Diagram 48.

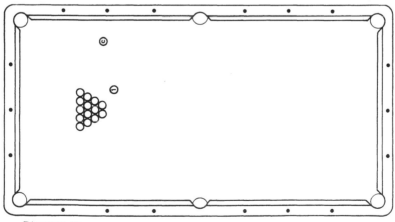

Diagram 49.

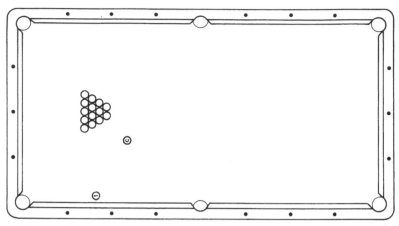

Diagram 50.

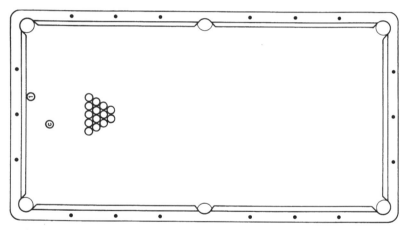

Diagram 51.

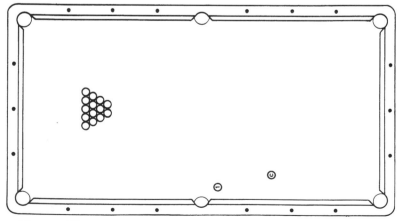

Diagram 52.

here is that these break shots recur in principle constantly throughout the game, no matter how many or few balls are left on the table. So if you're to play the game well, you'll have to learn how to look for them.

The break shot, then, is the heart of Straight Pool strategy. Let's take a look at the game's structure. We'll deal more here with the way the game goes, in terms of rules, than with how you deal with the various situations, although I'll give you a good start.

The opening break

The rules require the player breaking the balls to begin a game of Straight Pool to drive at least two object balls to a cushion after contact with the cue ball. What you want to do, of course, is follow the rule as closely as you can and drive *no more* than two balls out of the stack. (If you drive fewer than two to the rail, it's a two-point penalty and you have to try it again; or your opponent can play the balls as they lie, at his option; either way, you lose two points.)

A successful Straight Pool break can be accomplished with a softer stroke than you'd think, and I'd encourage you to develop confidence in breaking the balls softly. If you're breaking from the right-hand side of the stack, as most right-handers do, a modest amount of right-hand English is permissible; it will help compensate for your stroking the ball softly and enable you to get the cue ball back up near the head rail where it belongs. Diagram 53 shows you the opening break every player dreams of: two balls to the rail and back to safe areas, the cue ball back to the high country. This is always what you should strive for, of course, but you'll find it quite elusive.

The trick in breaking is to *aim*. Beginning players often assume that since they're not attempting to pocket anything on the break, it will suffice to send the cue ball off a *general area* of that corner object ball in the stack instead of a

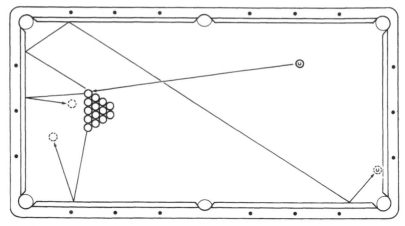

Diagram 53. The ideal opening break.

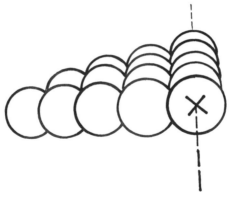

Diagram 54. Here's the hit you want.

specific point of aim. That is not correct. You want to strike the corner ball precisely on that point at which it lines up with the other four balls in its row, as in Diagram 54. That is the exact hit which will minimize object ball movement on the break; miss it by a flyspeck and, although the world won't necessarily come to an end, the results of your hit will be far less predictable. Small fractions of inches are critical in pool.

It would probably be a good idea (if admittedly a boring

one) for you to practice your Straight Pool break when there's no competition around. It takes some patience to re-rack the balls and walk around the table each time, but it will pay off. When the competition gets really good in Straight Pool, a careless opening break could cost you the whole rack, or 50 balls, or maybe even the whole game. It happens all the time when good players get it on.

Note, in Diagram 53, the line across the table behind which the cue ball begins the break. That's called the head string, and it figures prominently in the rules of the game later on. It's the imaginary line that runs between the respective second diamonds from the top on the long rails (some commercial rooms will have this line marked for you). And midway between the respective second diamonds from the *bottom* on the long rails is a point called the center spot (accurate but unimaginative); the first ball in any full 15-ball rack rests upon that spot, and any ball subsequently pocketed illegally (such as on a scratch shot) is brought back to that spot, or a place directly behind it.

Playing the game

Straight Pool awards you one point for every ball you pocket after first designating your choice of ball and pocket; in other words, you must call your shot. As a matter of courtesy, it isn't generally necessary to announce your obvious shots, but it's your responsibility to see that your opponent understands which shot you're trying.

If the ball you call goes in, and *other* object balls fall on the same shot (such as on shots where you break clusters apart), you get one point for each of those. And as long as the ball you call goes where you call it, it doesn't matter how, not even if it slops in there off other object balls or after another ball precedes it in. Any way you get it there counts.

In addition to that one point, of course, you get another

turn, and it should be pretty obvious that the objective in this or any other form of pool is to stay at the table longer than your opponent does. Pool reduces itself to the notion of successfully pocketing a ball *and* getting your cue ball someplace advantageous for a second shot. If you could do that every time you shot, you'd unseat every champion in history; but that's a little like telling a young baseball player that if he could swing at strikes only, he'd bat .600. It may be true in theory, but nobody's been able to do it yet.

So to stay at the table, you're going to have to learn and master the art of pool sequence. This is largely a mental process, one that comes easily to a lucky few and eludes the masses for years and years, often for good. But don't let that scare you; all the good players know sequence, at least to the extent of understanding what *should* be done even if execution breaks down now and then. And by now you're knee-deep into this book because you want to be a good player, right? Then you're well on the way already. You can learn pool sequence (1) if you *want* to badly enough, because it takes a level of concentration that few are accustomed to; and (2) if you go about it systematically.

You learn pool sequence by learning to evaluate the table layout in terms of work-to-be-done. Unless your opponent leaves you with a layout full of wide-open shots and nothing else, and you wouldn't want to sit on a hot stove waiting for *that* to happen, you'll have to decide which balls are pocketable without the cue ball's doing much else and which balls you might use as shots on which you break up remaining clusters, too. The phrase "work-to-be-done" equates with those balls which must be moved apart in order to render them pocketable.

Naturally, the more balls facing you on the table, the more complex your decision; but the game can always stymie you, even with as few as two object balls left to you. So your sequence decisions are not to be taken lightly, and once you achieve some skill with the basics of shotmaking, your talent for sequence will play a much larger role in your progress than your shotmaking. Granted, you've got to be able to get the ball in the hole before you can capitalize on your sequence skills, but the mechanics of shotmaking are available to you within a few weeks if you have any aptitude for the game at all. Sequence, as I've said, can take you forever. And if you're ever able to observe a player on the rise, you'll note that over the long run, it isn't his shotmaking that improves so colossally; it's just how much smarter he gets. Pocketing a ball is almost totally a matter of hand-eye coordination, the backbone of all sports. Once you display that, it's time to find out what you've got in your head to go with those good eyes. Pool, according to its experts, is 80 percent mental, and sequence represents the lion's share of that 80 percent.

I don't want to get you too deeply enmeshed in the mysteries of sequence in this book; just mastering the playing fundamentals represents a considerable challenge in itself. But learn to evaluate your table layouts in the manner I suggest, because that's the first step in determining position play. And never—*never*—take a shot wihout some form of plan as to what comes next. One lone pocketed ball isn't worth bus fare, unless it's the very last ball you need to win—*or unless it leads you to another one.* Beginners often fall into a fatal habit of let's-shoot-and-see-what-happens; that's the very first *playing* habit (as opposed to fundamentals habits) that you should avoid.

Consider Diagram 55 as an elementary exercise in sequence. The balls are numbered here in the order in which you should choose them, just to make it easier to follow, but what's most important is that you grasp the logic of *why* the sequence should run that way.

All the numbered balls are pocketable as they lie. But note that there's work to be done: that 11-ball cluster is going to have to be separated, at least partially, if your run is to continue beyond those 3 open balls.

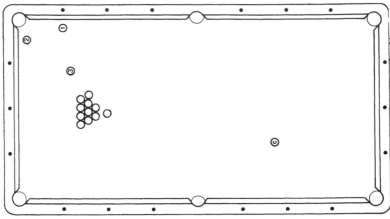

Diagram 55.

Which object ball now open to you will you use to break up that stack? The 3-ball, of course; not only is it closest to the massed balls (a good clue), but you can get to it logically in your sequence. The 2-ball could be shot first, but notice that position on the critical 3-ball will occur much more easily if you shoot the 1-ball first. If you shoot the 2-ball instead of the 1-ball, you'll have to measure the cue ball's speed off that bottom rail, and why give yourself one more thing to worry about? So you shoot the 1-ball softly, the cue ball rolls a few lazy inches to where you can shoot the 3-ball *and* break some of the other balls; *and* the 2-ball acts as a sort of safety valve that you can come back for if you don't like the outcome of your break.

As you can see, this may take a few words to explain, but the concept should occur to you much more quickly than that once you get comfortable about thinking pool. Eventually you'll find that at the peak of your game, your sequences are correct without your giving them much conscious thought at all.

Safeties

Once it's your turn, only three situations can force you to

surrender the table: you miss a shot, you're left with a situation that offers you nothing to shoot at, or you scratch (miss hitting any ball or put the cue ball in a pocket, or other ways we'll consider later). I'll assume you don't need me to explain what a missed shot is; so let's consider the other two circumstances, beginning with shotlessness and what you do about it.

The game is imitative of life, and you'll find some pretty reckless sorts in each. Some pool players have a reputation for firing at any remotely possible shot when they're seemingly stymied; others shun even mild risks and stick to what they're sure they can do. Whatever your life-style, I have a feeling that conservatism will serve you best at pool; the exception to that would be the rare player with *outstanding* shotmaking ability, who is not only capable of pocketing long, dangerous, off-angle shots but who can *count* on doing so. If that's how things work out for you, great, but it's more likely that your shotmaking will be something less than that. And I'm convinced that you'll do better to rely on your head than on your physical gifts.

So let's say that you don't have any shots, or at least you don't have any that you elect to take. You'll then be required to play a safety, and the legal requirements of that are that a ball must make contact with a rail following contact between cue ball and object ball. Which ball goes to the rail makes no difference; it's simply that cue ball or object ball must, after contact with each other, hit a rail. (You must also drive a ball to a rail on shots you *miss*, to avoid the penalty of a scratch.) The reason for this rule is pretty clear: if it didn't exist, virtually every game of pool would turn into a stalemate. A player would encounter a layout he didn't like, leave the cue ball where it was, and his opponent would do the same thing.

Diagram 56 shows you a reasonable example of sensible safety play. If the shooter were keen-eyed enough to cut the last coat of paint off that 1-ball, he *might* make it, and he'd

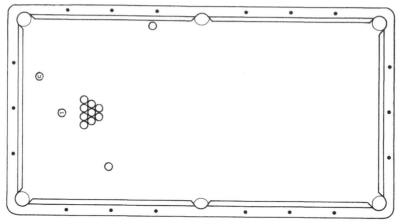

Diagram 56.

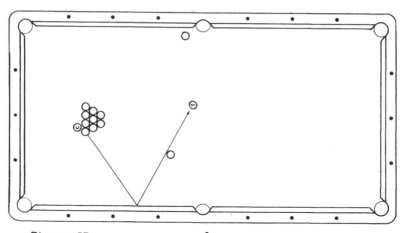

Diagram 57.

certainly splatter the stack. But the probability is too low to suit him, so he opts for the play of Diagram 57, driving the 1-ball to the rail and out of sight, hiding the cue ball against the bottom of the stack.

The best safeties do more than leave your opponent shot-less; they leave him without a way to play a return safety on you. Diagram 57, while not representative of a perfect safety, is pretty efficient; the incoming shooter is going to have to roll the cue ball someplace for a legal safety, and that is pretty sure to leave at least one of those loose object balls visible for a possible shot.

Safeties are the be-all and end-all of defensive play in pool, and you surely don't need to be told that in so many sports, the best offense is a good defense. It's not *quite* that important in pool; after all, you retain the offense as long as you can pocket balls. But its importance is underrated because when a table layout does stymie your opponent, it's your good safety play that will keep him on the defensive and give the first chance at an open shot to you rather than him.

The first step in learning to play sound defensive pool is to make the most accurate assessment you can of your shotmaking ability. Don't let shots intimidate you; on the other hand, don't take flyers, either. If you believe you can make a ball, shoot at it. If you don't, play a safety. And when you can't quite decide, play a safety then, too.

When possible, know your opponent's abilities as best you can, too. That will let you enlarge your repertoire to include safeties where you challenge him to shoot the do-or-die shots, leading to his miss and open shots for you.

A good safety should leave the cue ball someplace nasty: on or very near a rail, "jacked up" over another object ball, or buried in the stack. Don't feel guilty about doing this. Break-your-back safeties are the sign of a good player, not a bad person.

Scratches

How can you *lose* points in pool? Let me count the ways.

In tournament play, scratches are referred to more primly as "fouls," but the effect is the same: the penalized player loses at least one point and takes a seat. Here is your complete list of those infractions that constitute scratches.

When the opening break drives fewer than two object

balls to a rail after contact between the cue ball and the rack, the shooter goes two-in-the-hole (minus two, in other words) since the game is just beginning and no one has made any balls yet, and he can be made to break again. (Or, his opponent may elect to play the balls as they lie; either way, the two-point penalty stands.)

When the cue ball goes into a pocket, no matter what caused it to go there, the shooter loses any balls made on that shot, plus one off his existing score. And, naturally, he loses his turn.

When no ball touches a rail following cue ball-object ball contact, whether on a designated shot or a safety, the shooter loses a point and turn.

When the cue ball fails to contact an object ball at all, the shooter loses a point and turn.

When the cue ball jumps off the table, the shooter loses a point and turn. (But there's no penalty when an object ball does that.)

Any accidental movement of the cue ball, whether accomplished with cue, hand, or sleeve, costs the shooter a point and turn. In tournament play, they enforce this rule even more severely and call a foul if you disturb *any* ball in any way. But for practical day-to-day competition, it's generally "cue ball fouls only."

When you strike the cue ball more than once with the tip of your cue, that's another form of cue-ball foul. It happens when you're shooting at an object ball very close to the cue ball, and it usually leads to an argument. Unless you're playing a refereed game, you'll do well to ask an impartial third-party for a decision on this kind of foul.

And most awesome of all, the dreaded three-scratches rule: when a player loses two points on the opening break, he may be required to re-break as many times as necessary to meet the legal requirements, at two points per try. But once the game begins, any player who suffers any form of scratch in three consecutive turns at the table loses an additional 15 points (some tournaments now make this 25) and is required to re-break the balls as though the game were starting all over again. That means that you should always keep track of whether your opponent scratched in his last turn just before you took over the table. If he did, and you run into a shotless situation, you don't even have to play a legal safety; you just nudge the cue ball someplace totally unplayable and let him sweat it out. He's got to make a shot or complete a legal safety to get that scratch off his record—and he can't do what you just did, because that would be another scratch, and he'd be that much closer to three in a row. It's all right for you to have two consecutive scratches against you once he's made his third, because he has to break the balls then, and is very unlikely to leave you another scratch situation. So always remember who has the first scratch.

It's customary to make your opponent aware that he has two consecutive scratches against him at the time of the second scratch, and it helps avoid controversy if he then does stumble into a third scratch.

On scratches where the cue ball wanders into the pocket or leaves the table, the incoming shooter commences play with the cue ball anyplace he cares to place it down *behind that head string* we talked about earlier.

Re-racking the balls

As we mentioned, when play reduces the balls on the table to one, the other 14 are re-racked and play continues. The position of those re-racked balls is exactly as it would be if the 15th ball were there, occupying that center spot.

Now if that 15th ball interferes with the racking of the other 14 in the slightest way, it is to be moved to the head spot, which is, of course, in the center of the head string. That's important because a ball which is close to interfering with the re-racking is obviously also close to being a very good break shot, too. So when you're the shooter, closing out play in any given rack, be sure the ball you're saving for your break shot is in fact clear of the racking area. In the better rooms, the outline of the rack will be traced on the table so you can tell easily.

And that's Straight Pool in a nutshell. At any level of the game, any given play you see will correspond to one of the aspects we've just covered or variations of those, in varying sophistication. A simple game? Certainly not. To give chess its due for once, you could memorize in a matter of minutes how each piece may be legally moved and still not learn the game for centuries. That's the case with pool, too, and as you get into the game and uncover some of its depth and unpredictability, you'll see what a majestic game it really is. But always remember, the *simpler* you can make the game for yourself, the further you'll go. We've just covered the basics in reasonably simple terms, and I hope they get you off to the best playing habits in existence.

6

Eight-Ball

By all odds, this is the most popular of all pool games. It's always in vogue with beginners; it's the all-but-exclusive game of the pool leagues sprouting around the country, encompassing intermediate through advanced levels of play; and even the nation's topflight players are squaring off in a new proliferation of Eight-Ball tournaments.

How come, then, we didn't treat it first here as it might deserve? Because the best Eight-Ball players play the game like Straight Pool. They assess the work to be done, they plan sequences, they improvise just as Straight Pool players do. The difference is that only half the balls on the table, or fewer, are available to the shooter; but compensating him for that are all those extra balls for him to use as added defensive weapons.

Eight-Ball has lots of variations, too, which probably adds to its popularity. But the basic rules are pretty much the same: the balls are broken freely to start the game. If anything falls, the shooter continues. (Unless it's the 8-ball itself, in which case the game is lost. It used to be that you won the game for that, but not anymore. Don't ask me why.) If the ball he scored was a solid color—any number 1 through 7—he is committed to making those balls only for the duration of the game. If the first ball that falls is a stripe—or any number 9 through 15—the player is committed to making them. If one of each denomination falls on the break, the shooter continues at his option; the commitment will be determined by the next ball made. The commitment means that the shooter may only continue play if he continues to pocket what he's committed to; and he generally may not even play off his opponent's balls but rather must try to hit his own ball first. (Some people play anything goes, and it does make for a much more defensive game; but failure to hit one of your own balls with the cue ball before you touch anything else still costs you your turn in any case.)

Once a player has disposed of all seven of his balls, whether they were stripes or solids, he may shoot to pocket the 8-ball. He is required to call the shot—in other words, announce the pocket where he wants it. If he makes it there, he wins the game. If he misses, the game continues. If he scratches at all, whether the 8 goes in or not, he loses.

Again, don't be deceived; the rules are simple, but the game isn't. Eight-Ball is a rich little combination of some fairly sophisticated concepts from just about every other form of pool. But good Straight Pool players will become good Eight-Ball players almost without exception.

The break

You have to promise not to make this a permanent bad habit, but here's where upper-arm movement is permissible. You'll see a lot of players rearing back with their whole bodies, and leaping like Dr. J. to get into the stroke, but that's mostly wasted energy. Breaking pool balls is mostly a matter of quick hands, and you can get the job done quite well by limiting the movement of the break stroke to your arm. This will also make it easy for you to keep your head and bridge hand firm; after all, this isn't simply a wild-West blast, it's a stroke to be performed and aimed precisely like any other.

Place the cue ball on or just behind the spot in the middle of the head string; most tables will have it marked for you. Assuming the object balls are racked correctly, you'll have a straight line between your cue ball and the head ball in the rack. That is the line along which you should break. You want to nail that head ball right on the nose. I know you do better in bowling by hitting the side of the head pin, but this isn't bowling. If you miss that center hit by too much in this game, your cue ball will almost certainly head for one of the corner pockets. So hit the head ball head-on, stroking the cue ball in the center, nowhere else—and resist the temptation to wallop that cue ball just as hard as you can. You need some force to blast the balls apart, certainly, but you should transmit *no more speed to the cue ball than you can control.* Any break sufficient to move all 15 object balls gives you a pretty fair chance of pocketing one of them; when you hit the ball *harder* than what's required to do that, you might send some of the object balls on longer flights, but that doesn't necessarily mean that you improve your chances of pocketing them. Much more serious, when you turn the cue ball loose like that, you obviously don't know where it's going, and 15 flying missiles can do some awfully wicked things with it.

Correctly struck, your cue ball will smash that head ball and retreat toward the center of the table. You don't want it to follow on through the broken balls, because there's no telling where it will wind up; and you obviously don't want to draw it all the way back to the head rail, either. The proper combination of a center-ball hit dead on to the head ball and correct speed of stroke should cause your cue ball to die, or at least begin looking ill, once it gets to the center of the table.

Playing the game

Again, I believe the best attitude toward Eight-Ball is to play it like Straight Pool. That means you evaluate the layout of your remaining stripes or solids in terms of work to be done, and what most naturally leads to the next. Some of the object balls you need to pocket may well require liberating from small clusters; and since you'll generally be required to begin any shot by hitting one of your own balls first, you therefore must decide which of your object balls might lend themselves to shots in which you pocket one ball and break up others.

Most important of all, naturally, is the transition between the last object ball facing you and that black 8-ball. If you pocket your last stripe or solid, but either fail to get good position for the 8-ball or just plain miss it, you're up to your lower lip in quicksand. Not only have you missed a chance to win the game outright, but you've enhanced your chances of losing. Every single stripe or solid your opponent has left on the table represents one more chance for him to park the cue ball someplace playable for him but unplayable for you. Of course that doesn't mean that you should be hesitant about getting to the 8-ball first; that's the idea of the game. But I do want you to understand the importance of getting your win in one fell swoop from stripes or solids to the black ball, rather than hoping to win with a hiatus in between. Unless your opponent is juicily mediocre, that just won't happen.

7

Nine-Ball

This is pool's answer to Russian Roulette. Nothing much counts except what happens last.

Nine-Ball is a short, high-pressure version of the pool game called Rotation, which I've chosen not to treat in this book simply because hardly anybody plays it anymore. Both games require you to make contact with the lowest numbered ball on the table before the cue ball touches any other ball; once you complete that requirement, anything that goes in is good. The very best players, of course, don't trust luck that way. They just plan a sequence in numerical order and pocket the balls one by one.

In Rotation, you're awarded the points on any ball you pocket legally (one point for the 1-ball, two points for the 2-ball, etc.). The total number of points on all 15 balls is 120; so you win the game at the precise moment you total 61 or more.

But no such scorekeeping is required for Nine-Ball. You get no points for any balls. Nothing counts in the slightest way except the 9-ball. Make that any way at all, even luck-ily, and you win the game, as long as you make it with a legal shot; you may sink the 9-ball out of numerical rotation at any time as long as your shot begins by striking the lowest numbered ball available first.

If this seems a peculiar format for a friendly competitive game, you're on the right track. Nine-Ball is not all that friendly a game. You'll find it played in a tournament format, among experts, but Nine-Ball's almost total reason for being is as a gambling medium. Whoever makes the Nine-Ball wins a predetermined sum from his opponent or opponents; the game lends itself well to play by groups of players. No law says you *must* play the game for money, but Nine-Ball has a special pressure all its own which disappears during a sociable game and thereby makes the game much less interesting. It's very much like playing tennis without keeping score.

Nine-Ball is capable of telling you interesting things about the size of your Adam's apple. It's not uncommon at all to see players pocket the game's first eight balls with flair and verve and then have trouble guiding the 9-ball into a bushel basket.

The break

Let's talk first about how you rack the balls. You do that in a diamond pattern, the rows consisting of 1, 2, 3, 2, and 1 balls, as in Diagram 58. The 9-ball always goes in the cen-

Diagram 58. The Nine-Ball rack.

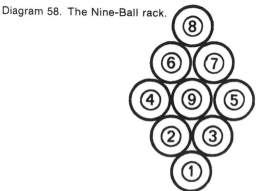

ter, just as the 8-ball does in Eight-Ball, where it is least likely to be pocketed (but it does happen, and in Nine-Ball, you win by making it on the break).

You break exactly as you do in Eight-Ball: a bang-on hit on the 1-ball with all the speed you can control. The break is considered a powerful advantage in Nine-Ball. Those two balls which flank the 9-ball in a Nine-Ball rack are the prime candidates to fall someplace, but whether they do or not, your chances for scoring are generally quite good if you break properly. You want the cue ball to do the same thing as in Eight-Ball: retreat to the center of the table and wait patiently for everything else to stop.

Playing the game

The first thing to note, naturally, is that your shot choice has been taken away from you. You must make the cue ball contact the lowest numbered ball on the table in some way before it hits any other ball. And of course you must count on leaving yourself a cue-ball position favorable to the next lowest ball on the table, too.

What remains to your discretion are the cue-ball routes you select to get you from ball to ball. To speak to that in the most general terms, you once again try to plan whatever's easiest; sometimes the layout will dictate itself to you, and that situation will become more frequent as your proficiency at the game improves. But don't count on that; Nine-Ball, like Eight-Ball, is deceptively complex. And since it's basically a gambling game, that's why it's always been a favorite haunt of hustlers, along with its obvious quickness.

The most common stymie you'll face in Nine-Ball is the snooker, or hook, in which case object balls interfere with the path between cue ball and the lowest numbered object ball (Diagram 59). These stymies may occur naturally off the break or as a result of your miscalculations in either planning or executing your plan; additionally, a skilled opponent may create them for you.

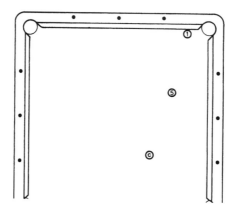

Diagram 59. One of Nine-Ball's typical hooks.

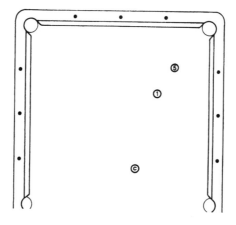

Diagram 60. Another of Nine-Ball's nasties.

Your defense against this unhappy quirk of fortune is a strategy called a rollout. As the name implies, you may roll the cue ball (usually just a few inches) to a point where a line to the correct object ball does exist. The price you pay for this strategy is that your opponent gets first crack at the shot you leave; he may opt to shoot it himself, or he may leave it there and challenge you to shoot it. In the latter case, you *must* hit the correct object ball with your shot, or your opponent is awarded the cue ball any place on the table he wants to put it. You can see that the ideal rollout is a "neither-nor" proposition. You can't leave anything easy, or your opponent will jump at the chance; and you can't leave anything too hard, or *you* won't be able to handle it. So you have to select a leave that's too hard for him but not for you, and that involves a skilled assessment of your own limits—and naturally it would be nice if you knew his, too.

The other major challenge of Nine-Ball occurs when higher number object balls interfere with the path of the correct ball to a pocket, rather than with the path between cue ball and object ball. Even though that interfering ball can theoretically be treated as a combination shot, don't fall for it; the probability of such shots is microscopically low, and worse than that, you don't have a clue as to where the *first* ball might end up, either. Unless the object balls are within a few inches of one another, you're much better off rolling out (perfectly legal) to a more practical position, or trying to "duck" either the initial object ball or the cue ball into a safety position; this kind of situation frequently represents an opportunity for you to "hook" the other guy by using that interfering ball to your advantage. That's a solution to the fix you see in Diagram 60: cut the 1-ball thin enough that it goes to the side rail and behind the 5-ball, with enough speed to get the cue ball back up the table.

Clearly, Nine-Ball requires you to think ahead. So does

every other form of pool, of course, but mental lapses are especially common in Nine-Ball because the shooter has his head fixed on going in numerical rotation and therefore takes his shot selection for granted. Don't fall for that, either. Always try to have a clear picture of how your next three shots will be negotiated, as a *minimum* plan. In a Nine-Ball game where the balls are being broken reasonably well, close to half of the resulting layouts will be playable to completion as they lie, given an open shot on the first ball; the rest will present some form of stymie. Since the stymie has to be dealt with somewhere along the way, let it be *you* who plans it out before you get to it, instead of the usually fatal I'll-worry-about-that-when-the-time-comes approach.

Speaking of that, you'd do well to learn not to trust luck in Nine-Ball. The lucky opportunities are certainly there, such as making the 9-ball on the break or slopping it in somewhere along the way by accident; but in the long run, the best player still wins. Unless you have a known superiority to your opponent and you're convinced he can't capitalize on your blunders anyway, *don't take flyers* just for the sake of rolling the 9-ball around. Be as precise as you can. Literally and figuratively, it will pay.

8

Two others

Straight Pool, Eight-Ball, and Nine-Ball are the three pool games that you'll commonly see played anywhere you go. What they have in common additionally is that all three games can be played and enjoyed between evenly matched players at all levels of skill, including the beginning-most beginners.

That is not the case with Bank Pool or One-Pocket, two other games which are almost exclusively played for stakes. Both are highly specialized games which make almost no sense and really aren't very much fun unless the players are advanced at least to the point of mastery of fundamentals. For that reason we won't go into them in any detail in this book, but they are played widely enough to rate a mention. Bank Pool, as you can probably tell, is a game in which only bank shots count; the shooter must designate ball and pocket and make his shot cleanly, without touching any second object balls. At the discretion of the players, scratches may or may not cost a point because of the difficulty of the game, and the first one to make eight banks wins.

In One-Pocket, only the two pockets at the foot of the table (nearest where the balls are racked) count for score, one for each player. The player breaking the balls designates his choice of pocket merely by choosing one side of the table from which to break; the opposite corner will be his. The first player to score eight balls in his pocket wins; balls falling into any of the other four pockets are re-spotted. One-Pocket is a game of supreme strategy, and defensive moves outnumber offensive ones by close to 3 to 1. Leave it alone until you're proficient in at least one other pool game.

There are two other games worth discussing, one to sharpen the physical aspects of your game, the other for the mental. They are, respectively, Cribbage and Golf.

Cribbage and Golf

In Cribbage, the balls are broken freely as in Eight-Ball. The objective is then to pocket two successive object balls having a combined face value of 15 (the 1-ball and 14-ball, for instance). No player may legally pocket the 15-ball until all the other object balls are gone. If a cribbage (balls with numbers combining to 15) is completed, those balls stay down and the shooter continues. If the player fails to complete a cribbage, any balls he pocketed are re-spotted and he yields his turn. Naturally, whoever makes the most cribbages wins.

Cribbage is really a pretty esoteric pool game, and if you were to stroll into a commercial room and start asking around for a Cribbage game, you'd be a stand-up comedy hit. The only reason I recommend it to you as a pool beginner is because of its emphasis on the relationship between two specific object balls. Remember the early two-ball drills I suggested when we discussed the fundamentals of shotmaking? Getting position on a specific second shot is ultimately what pool playing is all about. As I've said, if you can pocket a ball and position yourself for a second, nothing can stop you.

Cribbage will provide you with some incredible two-ball relationships, and of course while you're learning, you'd be well advised to select *simple* two-ball sequences with un-heroic shots available on each ball. But I think you'll find that you'll soon be able to branch out and make some position plays on a much more advanced plane, and the more you can learn, the better. The game will also help your safety play; safeties are quite legal, but now you'll have to think ahead and play your opponent safe on two object balls, not just one.

That's also why I think you might enjoy and benefit from Golf, a peculiar pool game played pretty much as the name suggests. You'll see it most commonly played between mul-tiple players for small stakes. The last is noteworthy be-cause pool's Golf is really something of a kibbitz; it's tre-mendous fun, and I don't think I've ever seen it played anywhere where at least one of the players wasn't cackling and whooping openly.

Each player is assigned his own object ball in Golf. Each player, in turn, begins the game by spotting his object ball and trying the same long bank shot at the pocket on his right. Once any player makes his ball there, it's re-spotted, and he sets about making it in the next pocket counter-clockwise around the horn. The first one to complete the "course" wins and collects from everybody; some games also make each player ante up nominally for each of his scratches, which can be plentiful, and the winner picks that up, too.

Sound simple? Ah, innocence. First of all, most intrepid Golfers play the game on a snooker table, much larger than the American pool table, which means that almost nobody opens up with a hole in one. Then there's the problem of your fellow players' object balls getting between your object ball and the pocket you need, and you don't ask anybody to "pick up" or "mark" in this game, you play it as it lies. If you scratch in any way, you go back one hole. You'll find yourself hooked where you can't get to your object ball, oh so many times. Getting your ball into either side pocket will seem like penance on the way to heaven. And most commonly, you'll find that to get your object ball anywhere near the pocket you need, you'll have to "kick" at it, which means driving the cue ball off a rail (sometimes plural rails) before it makes contact with your object ball.

Why fly over this cuckoo's nest in the first place? Well, you've already got one good reason: any game that can make you laugh out loud can't be all bad. Whatever your choice of game, at pool or anywhere else, I wouldn't play it for two seconds beyond the point at which it isn't fun. Golf is a more raucous kind of fun than the other pool games, but it's still great fun. Almost equally important, once you look at this game from the competitive point of view, it can show you just how crucial pool *thinking* is. Golf will take you through a fascinating series of "What if?" options, and once you gain some mental dexterity for them, your point of view for just about every other form of pool should be considerably refreshed. And once you do in fact become a better pool thinker, you can look for your game to take off and soar.

9

Game ball

By now the thread running through my approach to the game is pretty clear: successful pool playing is mostly a matter of reducing things to their simplest terms. In both concept and execution, I can't urge you strongly enough to *simplify*. It begins with your ability to hit the cue ball softly rather than hard, and goes on from there, right on through the most sophisticated pool played anywhere: those who go furthest in the game are those who do the most things simply.

The proof of this is waiting for you, very likely within a few weeks of now. If you pursue the game thoughtfully, as I've suggested throughout, and you have even a modest aptitude for it, you'll have your first legitimate run. How many balls are involved isn't important. What's significant is that it will occur to you, maybe even in mid-run, that you have strung the balls together correctly, without guessing or struggling, one thing leading logically to the next and to the next after that. For just the brief span of those six or eight or twelve or however many balls, you'll be aware of a terrifying feeling of mastery. You'll have taken the most difficult game man has devised yet and played it, however fleetingly, as well as anyone else could have. If you enjoy that kind of high enough, and I frankly can't see how you go about resisting it, the game will have reached you, and you're very apt to spend some time trying to claim that high for yourself again. You'll get it, too, and your runs should grow in length. But it's very much like a lot of other pleasurable things in life: the first time is always awfully special.

I hope you enjoy yours, and the incredible game of pool, for life.

Index

A

Accuracy, need for, viii
Aiming one's shot, 35-38, 39-41
  caroms, 60
  combination shots, 54-55
  kiss shots, 57-58
  straight pool, 65-66
Athletes, pool and, vii
Attitude, importance of, ix, 36
Awkward shots, 23-25

B

Balance
  cue, 4
  stance, 5, 6-7
Ball. *See* Cue ball; Object balls
Bank Pool, 87
Bank shots, 46-49, 50-53
  Bank Pool, 87
  Golf, 89
Baseball, pool and, 7-8, 9, 38, 68
Body types, effect on stance, 5
Bowling, pool and, 79
Boxing, pool and, 11

Break, 62-67
  Eight-Ball, 25, 77, 78-79
  Nine-Ball, 25, 82-83
  One-Pocket, 88
  re-racking, 76
  scratches, 73-74, 75
Break-your back safeties, 73
Bridge, mechanical, 9-10, 14
Bridges, grips, 14-24
Butt, of cue, 3
  grips and strokes, 12, 13, 14

C

Calling the shot, 67
  Eight-Ball, 78
Carom shots, 59-60
Center-ball hit, 42, 57-58
Center-ball play, 29, 39
Center spot, 67
Chalking, of cue tip, 3-4
Challenges, in Nine-Ball, 85
Champions, 8
  snooker, bridge used, 16
Chess, pool compared, vii-viii, 76

Clusters
  Eight-Ball, 80
  Straight Pool, 62, 69
Combination shots, 49, 53, 54–57
  Nine-Ball, 85
Comfort, in stance, 5–6, 7
Condition, physical, pool and, vii
Confidence, importance of, 33, 65
Consecutive pocketing, 41
Conservatism, advantages of, 71
Consistency, in stance, 9
Contact point, 33, 37
Control, importance of, 79
Corner ball, 65–66
Coordination, importance of, vii
Cradling, a cue, 13
Cribbage, pool game, 88–89
Cross-over banks, 50–51, 52–53
Crouching, 6
Crutch, 9
Cue
  aiming with, 38
  grips and strokes, 11–33
  height over, 5, 8–9
  level, 5–6, 8 16, 24
  owning one's own, 1–4
  striking ball twice, 74
Cue ball, 26–33, 91
  bridges, 18–21
  Eight-Ball, 79
  Golf, 90
  kill, 13
  Nine-Ball, 81, 83, 85
  pocketing with, 34–60
  Rotation, 81
  Straight Pool, 62, 65, 67, 68, 70–75
  stretching to reach, 9
Curving, of cue ball, 60
Cushion, 20, 65
"Cut" shots, 28, 35, 36, 39–40, 41, 42

D

"Dead" shot. 54

Defensive play, 60, 73
Deflection, of cue ball, 28
Diamonds, on rail, 29–30, 32, 67
"Draw", 28, 31, 33, 38, 49, 58–59
Draw, or tie, in pool, viii
Drills, 31–32, 41–42, 43–44, 88

E

East Coast, 62
Eight-Ball, 77–80
  bad way to learn pool, 25
  South and, 62
English, 28, 29, 33
  pocketing, 38–39, 42, 44, 49, 58–59
  Straight Pool, break, 65
Exercises, 26–33, 39, 43–44, 69–70

F

Feel, of cue, 3
Ferrule, of cue, 3
Firing a rifle, pool and, 6
Foot placement, stance, 5–10
Fouls, 73, 74
14.1 pocket billiards, 61, 62
Frozen balls, 20, 48, 54, 55
Fundamentals, importance, of, viii,
  11, 25

G

Gambling, Nine-Ball used for, 82, 88
Geographic distribution, 61–62
Golf, pool and, 11, 30–31
Golf, pool game, 80–90
Grips and strokes, 11–33
  balance, 4

H

Habits
  bad, 25, 69, 78
  good, 34, 76
Hand placement, grips and strokes.
  11–33

"Hard shot", 36
Head ball, in Eight-Ball, 79
Head spot, 75
Head string, 67, 75
    Eight-Ball, 79
Health, pool and, ix
Height over cue, 5, 8–9
Helmstetter, Dick, 2
"Hidden" shots, 45–46
Hook, in Nine-Ball, 83–85
Hoppe, Willie, grip, 13–14
House cue, 2, 3

I

Ideal stroke, 24–25
Indirect shots, 45–46
Infinity, in pool, viii
Infractions. *See* Scratches

J

Janes, Danny, 2
Japan, cues, 2

K

Kiss shots, 57–59

L

Ladies' aid, 9'
Lassiter, Luther "Wimpy", 62
Layouts, 68, 69, 71, 73
    Eight-Ball, 80
    Nine-Ball, 86
Length, of cue, 3
Level cue, 5–6, 8, 16, 24
Long banks, 49, 50, 52–53
Loop, in bridge, 16–17, 18, 19, 20

M

Masse shot, 60
Mechanical bridge, 9–10, 14
Meucci, Bob, 2

Minnesota Fats, quoted, 4
Miscue, 4, 28
Mizerak, Steve, 8
Mosconi, Willie, 8
Muhammad Ali, 11

N

Natural bank shots, 46–47
Nine-Ball, 81–86
    bad way to learn pool, 25
    caroms, 60
    South and, 62

O

Object balls
    Bank Pool, 87
    Cribbage, 88, 89
    Eight-Ball, 79, 80
    Golf, 89–90
    Nine-Ball, 85
    pocketing, 34–60
    Straight Pool, 62, 65–66, 70, 73–74
One-Pocket, 87, 88
"On" shot, 54
Opening break, in Straight Pool, 65–67
    scratches, 73–74
Open-thumb bridge, 16, 23–24
"Opposite-spin" effect, 39, 58
Owning one's cue, 1–4

P

Parallel-the-rail shots, 23–24
Penalties. *See* Scratches
Pendulum stroke, 25
Perfect stroke, 25
Personality, reflected in pool, viii–ix
Physical condition, pool, and, vii
Placement
    feet (stance), 5–10
    hands (grips and strokes), 11–33
Pocketing, 34–60

Point of balance, of cue, 4
Point of contact, 33, 37
Points, in scoring 67–68
  Bank Pool, 87
  Rotation, 81
  scratches, 73–75
Position play, 69
Practice, 41–42, 43
  strokes, 30–31
Prices, of cues, 1–2
Psyching, 8

R

Rack, 61, 62, 67
  Eight-Ball, 79
  Nine-Ball, 82–83
  re-racking, 75–76
Rails, 43–44, 70
  "cut" shots and, 41
  diamonds on, 29–30, 32, 67
  Golf, 90
  opening break, 65, 67
  safeties, 71, 73
  scratches, 71, 74
  shooting away from 20, 22–24
Rake, 9
Refereed game, 74
Re-racking, 75–76
Rifle, firing, pool and, 6
Rollout, in Nine-Ball, 85
Rotation, form of pool, 81
  caroms, 60
  draw, or tie, viii
Russo Interlocking Bridge Head,
  9–10

S

Safeties, 70–73
  Cribbage, 89
  Nine-Ball, 85
  scratches. 74. 75

Schrager, Bert, 2
Scratches, 71, 73–75
  Bank Pool, 87
  center spot, 67
  Eight-Ball, 78
  Golf, 89, 90
Sequence, pool, 68–70
  Cribbage, 89
Shaft, of cue, 3
Shooting off a rail, 23–24
Short-angle cross-over bank 50–51
Short banks, 49
Short games, 61, 62
Side pocket shot, 36–37
Simplicity, importance of, viii
  11–12, 24–25, 76, 91
Snooker, game, 16
  table, 89
Snooker, or hook, in Nine-Ball
  83–85
South, pool and, 61–62
Spain, Burton, 2
Spin, 28, 29, 38–39, 42, 58
Squeezing, the cue, 13
Stack, 65, 70, 72
Stance, 5–10
"Stepping in the bucket", 7–8
Stopping, cue ball, 28
Straight, or straight-in, shot, 36, 38
  39, 42, 44
"Straight-back" bank, 50, 52
Straightness, of cue, 3
Straight Pool, 61–76
  caroms, 60
  Eight-Ball and, 77
Strength, pool and, vii
Stretching, 9, 10
Strokes and grips, 11–33
  balance, 4
Stroud, Bill, 2
Suppliers, of cues, 2
Szamboti. Gus. 2

T

Taper, of cue, 3
Tennis, pool and, 11, 33
Thickness, of cue, 3
Three-ball shots, 56–57
Three-scratches rule, 74–75
"Throw" effect, of English, 42
Tip, of cue, 3–4, 74
Tournaments, 61
   Eight-Ball, 77
   Nine-Ball, 82
   scratches, 73, 74, 75

Tripod bridge, 17
Two-in-the-hole, 74

U

Underspin, 38

V

Vertical spin, 28

W

Weight, of cues, 2
Wobbles, in cue, 3